100 THINGS TO DO IN SAN DIEGO BEFORE YOU DIE

3rd Edition

Ferry to Coronado Island

3rd Edition

100 THINGS TO DO IN SAN DIEGO BEFORE YOU DIE

DAVID SWANSON

REEDY PRESS

Reedy Press
PO Box 5131
St. Louis, MO 63139, USA
reedypress.com

Library of Congress Control Number: 2025936760

ISBN: 9781681065953

Design by Jill Halpin

Cover photo courtesy of David Swanson.

Printed in the United States of America
25 26 27 28 29 5 4 3 2 1

CONTENTS

Music and Entertainment

Sports and Recreation

Culture and History

Shopping and Fashion

PREFACE

As a third-generation San Diegan, I grew up living the quintessential California dream: beaches at my front door, lemon trees and rosemary bushes outside the pantry, and mountains and desert in my backyard. While I exaggerate—slightly—the proximity of these natural assets, there's no question that we are blessed with an outstanding location, and our benevolent, Mediterranean climate allows San Diegans to embrace an outdoor lifestyle year-round.

I've watched the city evolve from the conservative surfer-and-sailor town of my childhood into a vibrant city with an economy that fires on all cylinders, as new tech and health industries find synergy with the established ones like education and defense. Over the last quarter century, an influx of fresh talent has provided an infusion of new energy, ideas, and money to nourish cultural institutions, fuel our dining and nightlife, and rejuvenate older, run-down neighborhoods. Today, we celebrate a well-funded San Diego Symphony (California's oldest), a San Diego restaurant that was the first in Southern California to earn Michelin three-star ranking (Addison), and neighborhoods such as South Park and Barrio Logan that have become enticing draws for locals and visitors alike.

Humming in the background is tourism, the lifeblood of the city. I've been writing about travel to San Diego since 1995, and compiling the third edition of this book has reminded me of activities I hadn't explored in years. But it also introduced me to new discoveries I was excited to find—and to now share with you. In narrowing the list to a nice, round hundred, I strived for a geographical spread that kept a focus on neighborhoods in the core city but also included a handful of recommendations that lie at the edges of San Diego County—30, 40, or more miles from downtown. And although there are certainly spendy experiences to be treasured (hot air balloon ride, anyone?), you'll find lots of free or gently priced activities and meals celebrated in these pages.

As always, the assistance of the knowledgeable team at the San Diego Tourism Authority provided suggestions and fact-checking help at crucial points. My immediate San Diego family—Anthony, Sarah, Erik, Denise, Kyle and Eva, Hayley and Chanelle—offered input that helped me narrow the list at several points, whether they knew it or not. And Chris kept the home fires burning—always supportive, always organized, always loving. Thank you, all.

Now, pack a laid-back attitude along with your sandals and swimsuit (and a sweater for those cool summer evenings!), and let's uncover the best of California's grown-up beach town.

San Diego Zoo

Tribute Pizza

FOOD AND DRINK

1

BITE INTO SAVORY T. J.-STYLE TACOS

AT PUESTO

You came here for the tacos, right? San Diego and Tijuana are joined at the hip, so it only makes sense that San Diego's favorite food is omnipresent and celebrated everywhere, from food trucks to corner taco shops, and from cherished Mexican restaurants to luxe gourmet eateries. Local chain Puesto has covered the bases well since its start, and the taco focus is bounding from strength to strength. Start with an order of crudo or ceviche and one of the three different guacamoles—take note that Puesto uses organic non-GMO blue corn tortillas and mixes margaritas with additive-free agave spirits. The restaurant's "crispy cheese" tacos include the usual suspects, like chicken al pastor and carnitas, but make room for the delicious mushroom taco with pickled onions and a stone fruit salsa, or the CDMX rib eye taco with escabeche, ash salsa, and avocado salsa.

789 W Harbor Dr., downtown, 619-233-8880
5010 Mission Center Rd., Mission Valley, 619-333-2167
1026 Wall St., La Jolla, 858-454-1260
eatpuesto.com

TIP

Throughout San Diego, Taco Tuesday is honored like a religious holiday, even at restaurants not focused on south-of-the-border menus. Anticipate taco deals—and at Old Town's Mexican venues, expect crowds.

MORE PLACES TO CHOW DOWN CALI-BAJA TACOS

Tacos el Gordo

511 F St., downtown, 619-955-8220
tacoselgordobc.com

Lola 55

1290 F St., downtown, 619-542-9155
7720 El Camino Real, Carlsbad, 760-274-6309
lola55.com

Fish Guts

2222 Logan Ave., Barrio Logan, 619-888-0081
fishgutscalifornia.com

Oscar's Mexican Seafood

646 University Ave., Hillcrest, 619-230-5560
746 Emerald St., Pacific Beach, 858-412-4009
oscarsmexicanseafood.com

City Tacos

3028 University Ave, North Park, 619-296-2303
8325 La Mesa Blvd., La Mesa, 619-467-7999
1031 S Coast Hwy. 101, Encinitas, 760-230-1385
4516 Mission Blvd., Pacific Beach, 858-284-4239
citytacossd.com

2

RISE TO THE OCCASION
AT WAYFARER BREAD

Inhabiting a small former taco stand in La Jolla's Bird Rock neighborhood, behind a terrace topped by passion fruit vines, Wayfarer crafts bread that will make you think you've landed in the heart of France. The artisinal sourdough loaves emerge from the oven crackling, with an almost-burnt hue that reveals itself to be a caramelized crust. The naturally fermented breads are only half the story. There are painstakingly produced French-inspired pastries—the humble croissants go through a three-day birthing, which is why they taste perfect. When the vines ripen in late summer, watch for passion fruit cream buns, in which the fruit and cream cheese are folded into a croissant. You'll find savory pastries like a traditional ham and cheese croissant, plus a Wayfarer invention: croissant tiles (a pastry boat that cradles a cheese and seasonal veggie combo). At 11:00 a.m. each morning, two grab-and-go sandwiches are available—one veggie, the other with meat. But come early: Everything is small batch and items run out when they run out.

5525 La Jolla Blvd., La Jolla
wayfarerbread.com

FLUFF AND FOLD
AT AN'S DRY CLEANING

Yes, from the outside it looks just like a neighborhood dry-cleaning shop—the kind of business you could pass by for years without ever pondering what goes on inside. But after it reopened in 2018 as an ice cream store, patrons started to line up out the door for gelato in a variety of unusual flavors. There's Fedora, inspired by the traditional tiramisu dessert, swirled with mascarpone, coffee, cognac, and lumps of sponge cake. The surprisingly subtle and creamy Canvas is infused with rosemary and mixed with olive oil, while Full Grain Leather uses brown butter in the gelato base and swirls in brookies (brownie cookies). The line moves glacially, but that's because everyone gets a taste of all seven flavors on the rotating menu. An has done so well in the dry-cleaning business that she's been trying her hand at other trades. If the original location isn't convenient, try An's Athletic Field Services (downtown), An's Electronic Repair (Ocean Beach), and An's Hatmakers (Del Mar); each with its own menu of ice cream.

3017 Adams Ave., North Park, 619-450-6166
adcgelato.com

4

CHOOSE YOUR TEMPERATURE
AT RARE SOCIETY

I don't find national steak house chains to be all that appealing, steeped as they are in posturing and predatory pricing. At Rare Society, chef Brad Wise hit on a winning combination of quality cuts, generously seasoned, and an unpretentious ambience that speaks to neighborhood and community rather than out-of-towners with expense accounts. The original Uptown location is my go-to, but a second location in Solana Beach opened in 2022 and proved so popular that Rare Society found the recipe to go national (fingers crossed the local flavor survives). Start with a dynamite Caesar salad that puts Parmesan, garlic, and anchovy right up front, or perhaps a seafood tower heaped with oysters, snow crab claws, ahi tuna tartare, Maine lobster, and more. But you came for the steaks, and whether you invest in filet mignon, Snake River Farms Wagyu tri-tip, a pork tomahawk, or my personal favorite, the Cedar River prime bullseye rib eye, you won't go wrong. It's a special evening out.

4130 Park Blvd., University Heights, 619-501-6404
330 S Cedros Ave., Solana Beach, 858-771-0181
raresociety.com

MY OTHER STEAKHOUSE FAVORITES

Cowboy Star Restaurant and Butcher Shop

Western-inspired, contemporary and sophisticated.
640 Tenth Ave., downtown, 619-450-5880
cowboystar.com

Born and Raised

Great Gatsby styling and decadent tableside preparations.
1909 India St., Little Italy, 619-202-4577
bornandraisedsteak.com

Island Prime

Steaks with a swell view.
880 Harbor Island Dr., Harbor Island, 619-298-6802
islandprime.com

Turf Supper Club

Grill your own at this retro neighborhood pick; open late.
1116 25th St., Golden Hill, 619-234-6363
turfsupperclub.com

Bully's East Prime Bistro Sports Bar

Old-school sports bar and local favorite for prime rib.
2401 Camino del Rio S., Mission Valley, 619-291-2665
bullyseastsd.com

5

DROP ANCHOR FOR FRESH CATCH
AT THE FISHERY

From the early 1900s through the 1970s, America's tuna fishing and canning industry was based in San Diego, making the city the "tuna capital of the world." While the industry has moved overseas, a commercial fishing fleet still thrives, with the freshest catch often winding up on local tables. I like the Fishery, which has evolved from a simple fish counter featuring sustainable, wild-caught local fish into one of San Diego's finest, freshest seafood restaurants. Fish is the only protein on the weekly changing menu, but choices might include rock crab bucatini, a vermilion rockfish served whole, or Saltspring Island mussels in green curry. Chef-partner Mike Reidy visited London several times to get the batter right for a succulent fish and chips dish that never rotates off the menu. The polished warehouse setting invites casual dining, especially at lunch, when an albacore tuna salad sandwich is served up.

5040 Cass St., Pacific Beach, 858-272-9985
thefishery.com

6

HAVE A GAY OLD TIME
AT URBAN MO'S BAR & GRILL

Hillcrest has been the epicenter of LGBTQ culture in San Diego dating back to at least the late 1950s; by the 1970s, the city birthed its annual Gay Pride Parade, which travels through Hillcrest to Balboa Park. A mainstay for the community has been Mo's which, for more than 30 years, has been a "homo" away from home for the community and its allies. Whether you come for breakfast and brunch favorites such as country fried steak and eggs or spicy chilaquiles and eggs or arrive for the lunch and dinner menu of salads, sandwiches, burgers, and Cajun blackened chicken, the food is reliable and the mood is always cheerful. But what really draws the crowd is a roster of fun events such as Babette's Bingo, themed trivia contests, an all-you-can-eat spaghetti and showtunes event, and various drag revues. Come one, come all, but come as you are to Mo's and you'll be welcomed.

308 University Ave., Hillcrest, 619-491-0400
urbanmos.com

TIP

Today, San Diego's Pride festivities are celebrated annually over a weekend in mid-July that draws more than 250,000 attendees for the parade and festival.

7

EAT THE FARM
AT A. R. VALENTIEN

When Berkeley chef Alice Waters introduced the "farm-to-table" concept at her groundbreaking restaurant Chez Panisse, few cities in the US could better embrace such a sensible cooking trend as San Diego, where year-round farms dot the backcountry, providing a wide variety of produce within an hour or two of the cutting board. Executive Chef Kelli Crosson's market-inspired menu at A. R. Valentien is dictated by the season. Classic dishes like chicken liver pâté, duck confit, a Brandt beef prime rib eye, or white wine–braised Northern halibut share the plate with such delicacies as preserved Meyer lemons, charred heirloom carrots, Chioggia beets, and morel mushrooms—all tasting more rich and ambrosial than we mortals have any right to expect. The setting is the handsome and gracious Lodge at Torrey Pines, a Craftsman-style golf resort, in a room adorned with stained glass, metal-wrapped wood beams, and plein air paintings of Southern California landscapes.

11480 N Torrey Pines Rd., Torrey Pines, 858-777-6635
lodgetorreypines.com/ar-valentien

SCAN THE DRAMATIC BAY AND SKYLINE VIEW
AT C LEVEL

No restaurant offers a better perch for taking in the San Diego Bay and downtown skyline panorama than C Level—full stop. Located on Harbor Island, a man-made peninsula close to the San Diego Airport, C Level manages to put newcomers right in the San Diego spirit, which is why it's a favorite of mine after picking up visitors at the airport. A seat on the outdoor terrace rewards with front-row views of transiting cruise and navy vessels. The California-Med menu has something for everyone, but winning dishes include the ahi, crab and avocado stack, the kale and prosciutto salad, and the "everything" crusted ahi. Skirts on Fire lands a spicy skirt steak and blue cheese atop a zesty salad. While C Level can be packed at sunset, especially for the weekday happy hour, it's always a great spot for lunch.

880 Harbor Island Dr., Harbor Island, 619-298-6802
cohnrestaurants.com/islandprime

TIP

The adjacent Island Prime steakhouse and neighboring high-end Cali-Baja restaurant Coasterra—both also overseen by C Level's chef-partner Deborah Scott—offer essentially the same CinemaScope view, but I have a slight preference for the unimpeded vista from C Level.

9

HONOR RENOWNED PIES OF THE WORLD
AT TRIBUTE PIZZA

San Diego is regularly named by TripAdvisor as one of America's top cities for pizza. While New Yorkers may scorn, San Diegans, well . . . keep eating craft pizzas, content to keep the Neapolitan creativity flowing. Occupying the Art Deco former North Park post office, Tribute Pizza's menu pays homage to fine pies around the world, such as the Lady Diavola (crafted by 360 Degrees Artisan Pizza in Nairobi, Kenya), the Mushroom Whitestone 2.0 (from San Diego's own Bronx Pizza), and of course, the classic Margherita, as invented by Pizzeria Brandi (Naples, Italy). A few are topped by Mike's hot honey, others with organic crushed tomatoes from Bianco Dinapoli, and there is a plant-based and vegan menu. Ask about seasonal specialties—in summer, look for the refreshing stone fruit panzanella salad.

3077 North Park Way, North Park, 619-450-4505
tributepizza.com

OTHER SPOTS FOR TASTY CRAFT PIZZAS

Buona Forchetta

3001 Beech St., South Park, 619-381-4844
2865 Sims Rd., Liberty Station, 619-548-5770
1000 C Ave., Coronado, 619-675-0079
buonaforchettasd.com

Isola Pizza Bar

1526 India St., Little Italy, 619-255-4230
isolapizzabar.com

Blind Lady Ale House

3416 Adams Ave., North Park, 619-255-2491
blindladyalehouse.com

Caffé Calabria

3933 30th St., North Park, 619-291-1759
caffecalabria.com

Bronx Pizza

111 Washington St., Hillcrest, 619-291-3341
bronxpizza.com

Ambrogio15

26 Turquoise St., Pacific Beach, 858-291-8650
ambrogio15.com

10

QUAFF CRAFT SUDS
AT STONE BREWING WORLD BISTRO

San Diego's beloved beer giant Stone Brewing—the brewery best known for trailblazing the West Coast Style IPA—is also noted for two restaurants serving creative pub fare in handsomely designed settings. The globe-girdling menu ranges from Kung Pao crispy brussels sprouts to katsu chicken salad, steak frites, burgers, tacos, and Stone's Buenaveza Lager beer-battered fish and chips. A rotating draft list of more than 40 beers includes special-release Stone brews not available elsewhere, along with a rotating selection from other fine breweries. The 600-seat venue at Liberty Station in Point Loma sprawls into a rock-studded garden with waterways, a bocce ball court, and an outdoor cinema. Be aware that the restaurant lies right in the airport's flight path—a sure conversation stopper—but indoor seating is also available. At the Escondido location, 45 minutes north of downtown, you can visit the original brewery before or after dining, with tours available at 2:00 and 4:00 p.m. daily.

2816 Historic Decatur Rd., Point Loma, 619-269-2100
1999 Citracado Parkway, Escondido, 760-294-7866
stonebrewing.com/visit/bistros

OTHER GREAT BREWPUBS FOR CRAFT BEER LOVERS

Blind Lady Ale House (Automatic Brewing)

3416 Adams Ave., Normal Heights, 619-255-2491
blindladyalehouse.com

Ballast Point

2215 India St., Little Italy, 619-255-7213
ballastpoint.com

Coronado Brewing

170 Orange Ave., Coronado, 619-437-4452
1205 Knoxville Street, Bay Park, 619-275-2215
coronadobrewing.com

Pizza Port

1956 Bacon St., Ocean Beach, 619-224-4700
204 Palm Ave., Imperial Beach, 619-373-1470
135 N Hwy. 101, Solana Beach, 858-481-7332
571 Carlsbad Village Dr., Carlsbad, 760-720-7007
pizzaport.com

Karl Strauss Brewing Co.

1157 Columbia St., downtown, 619-234-2739
9675 Scranton Rd., Sorrento Mesa, 858-587-2739
5801 Armada Dr., Carlsbad, 760-431-2739
karlstrauss.com

11

RAISE THE BAR ON CRAFT COCKTAILS

AT RAISED BY WOLVES

A suburban mall is not where you'd normally look for the most unusual bar in the city, and yet there you'll find Raised by Wolves, idling quietly along a nondescript passageway at Westfield UTC. By day, it's a bottle shop, but one look at the curated selection of rare spirits posing behind polished glass and you'll know this is no ordinary liquor store. By late afternoon the boutique's fireplace becomes a secret passageway into an ornate hideaway bar. In style, it's part French Art Nouveau and part Art Deco, with a healthy dash of Disney staging to set jaws agape. The circular bar sits beneath a domed, stained glass ceiling, an ornate water fountain at its center, and bartenders mix riffs on a litany of classic cocktails, creating unexpected, often ambrosial elixirs. Make a reservation, and prepare to be delighted.

4545 La Jolla Village Dr., #2030, La Jolla, 619-629-0243
raisedxwolves.com

12

DINE WITH YOUR HEAD IN THE (MICHELIN) STARS

AT ADDISON

San Diego chefs long lamented the lack of respect their restaurant scene receives on the national stage. The ongoing oversight started to dissolve in 2019, when Addison became the city's first restaurant to be recognized with a star from Michelin, the world's oldest restaurant guide. Two years later a second star was awarded, and in 2022 Addison received a third—before any other venue in Southern California had been so honored. Sitting amid the sumptuous grounds of the Fairmont Grand Del Mar resort, the kitchen is under the direction of Executive Chef William Bradley. Count on 22-karat gold trimmings, percolating fireplaces, formal ambience, and doting service. The menu is seasonally inspired contemporary California cuisine, which might include a chicken liver churro, or Regiis Ova Reserver caviar with Koshihikari rice and smoked sabayon, or Cantonese quail with a five-spice sauce. At the time of this book's publication, the 10-course tasting runs $385 per person.

5200 Grand Del Mar Way, Carmel Valley, 858-314-1900
addisondelmar.com

13

SAVOR MEXICO
AT CASA GUADALAJARA

One cuisine tops the list for most San Diego visitors: Mexican. While there are dozens of decent Mexican restaurants and hundreds of taco shops throughout the city, it's not easy to identify one standout that delivers a menu with a wide variety of options (including vegetarian), tasty food, and a festive, memorable ambience—but sitting at the front of the line is Casa Guadalajara. The restaurant has an inviting outdoor patio with burbling fountains under a giant pepper tree, or you may choose to dine indoors with the piñatas. On weekend evenings you'll be serenaded by mariachis as you sample copious portions of traditional and regional Mexican specialties, such as *cochinita pibil*—Yucatan pork baked in achiote and orange juice, with pickled red onions and yellow chiles. Regardless of when you visit, the *abuelas* roll out the dough for tortillas and fresh chips, the margaritas are birdbath-sized, and the waitresses are adorned in ruffled, embroidered dresses.

4105 Taylor St., Old Town, 619-295-5111
casaguadalajara.com

LOAF ABOUT
AT BREAD & CIE

The scent of baking bread permeates this beloved Hillcrest bakery and café, where the traditions of artisanal European bread-making are practiced daily. Every loaf is made with organic flour and natural starters for leavening, with careful attention to the fine points of texture and crust. The result is bread that is served at dozens of the city's best restaurants. More than 20 different breads are baked daily, and others rise to the roster just once or twice a week (my fave: the deliciously meaty walnut and scallion). There's a monthly changing show of local artworks on the walls and a decidedly European clientele, and you don't have to be a batard booster to enjoy the house-made granola, the elegant tarts and scones for breakfast, or the Mediterranean-inspired soups and sandwiches at lunch.

350 University Ave., Hillcrest, 619-683-9322
breadandcie.com

15

HARVEST VINE-RIPENED FRUIT AT CARLSBAD STRAWBERRY COMPANY

San Diego County is one of the nation's most important farm economies—it has more small farms than any other county, and it's among the top producers of avocados, lemons, and tomatoes. We're also in the top 10 for strawberries, and the Carlsbad Strawberry Company's 40-acre farm has been growing the berries for four generations in a field sitting between Interstate 5 and the Batiquitos Lagoon. Strawberries are the first fruit to ripen in the new year, so the harvest usually starts in late January. Better yet, pick your own starting in February or March (once the fields are less muddy), and continue to do so through early July. The county's temperate climate and abundant sunshine make for deliciously sweet strawberries, so take your time while walking through the fields to look for the ripest ones. Remember, those buckets fill up fast!

1050 Cannon Rd., Carlsbad, 760-603-9608
carlsbadstrawberrycompany.com

KISS THE HIGH TIDE
AT THE MARINE ROOM

A San Diego icon since 1941, the Marine Room sits at the shore's edge, a barely legal location today. Most evenings, tides roll across the sand lazily, the water gently lapping at the building. But during unusually high summer tides, dinner beside the restaurant's wall-to-wall windows can be quite a thrill, with waves crashing against the glass between every bite. Fortunately, the food, a decadent (and *très cher*) marriage of Mediterranean and Asian, lives up to the spectacle, with such favorites as local bluefin tuna tataki and grilled swordfish along with prime cuts from Creekstone Farms and a cauliflower romanesco steak. There's also a lounge for cocktails, caviar, and a raw bar. Ideally, schedule your reservation an hour or so before high tide—if you're lucky, it coincides with sunset—to enjoy the scampering sandpipers and fishing pelicans before the parade of illuminated rollers arrives to splash your view.

1950 Spindrift Dr., La Jolla Shores, 858-459-7222
marineroom.com

SLICE INTO
A CLASSIC JULIAN APPLE PIE

The Julian Pie Company, founded in 1986, was born while Liz Smothers was peeling apples and baking pies for a local pie shop. As her pie-making services became more in demand, Smothers decided to start her own business in Julian, a mountain community of 1,500 residents. With apples and other fruit coming from local orchards, the pies became renowned for their flaky golden crust, and today they're shipped around the country. Among more than 20 different types, the number-one seller is Dutch apple, with other favorites being apple mountain berry crumb, pecan, and strawberry-rhubarb; sugar free pies are also available. The mountain town is a delight to discover, but if you don't want to make the trek to Julian, a 90-minute drive from downtown, a number of San Diego grocers sell fresh or frozen Julian Pies, including most Vons supermarkets.

2225 Main St., Julian, 760-765-2400
julianpie.com

INDULGE
IN EXTRAORDINARY DESSERTS

Truth in advertising: The desserts at this cherished institution are to die for (though not before you check off the other 99 things cited in this book!). Pastry chef–owner Karen Krasne has been satisfying San Diego's sweet tooth since 1988, as well as our cravings for butter cream, Valrhona chocolate, and garnishings of fruit, rose petals, and gold leaf. Krasne, who has trained with French masters at Cordon Bleu, Lenôtre, and Pierre Hermé, specializes in decadent cakes—sold whole or by the generous slice—as well as scones, tarts, brownies, Napoleons, and, well, the list goes on, many of them marked by unusual flavor combinations. Both locations offer a satisfying savory menu, including paninis, grilled cheese, soups, salads, and delicious charcuterie and cheese plates. The teas and coffees are nicely chosen, and beer and wine are also on offer.

2870 Fourth Ave., Bankers Hill, 619-294-2132
1430 Union St., Little Italy, 619-294-7001
extraordinarydesserts.com

MANGIA! MANGIA!
AT CUCINA URBANA

San Diego is full of solid Italian restaurants, especially in busy Little Italy, but the popular Cucina Urbana, Tracy Borkum's celebration of hearty, farm-style fare, is my favorite. The large venue is creatively furnished in both custom and reclaimed elements, such as odd light fixtures and vintage Italian movie posters—it's like a rustic farmhouse with an artistic bent. The menu evolves seasonally, but staples include a memorable chopped Italian salad, tempura fried squash blossom stuffed with goat cheese and orange blossom honey, and a dynamite bucatini amatriciana. There are creative Neapolitan pizzas, and the half chicken frá diavolo with mascarpone polenta will knock your socks off. Grab a bottle in the restaurant's wine shop and take advantage of the modest corkage fee.

505 Laurel St., Bankers Hill, 619-239-2222
urbankitchengroup.com/cucina-urbana-bankers-hill

ITALIAN RESTAURANTS IN LITTLE ITALY (AND BEYOND) WORTH DISCOVERING

Bencotto

750 W Fir St, Little Italy, 619-450-4786
lovebencotto.com

Civico 1845

1845 India St., Little Italy, 619-431-5990
civico1845.com

Barbusa

1917 India St., Little Italy, 619-238-1917
barbusa.com

Ciccia Osteria

2233 Logan Ave., Barrio Logan, 619-674-4069
cicciasandiego.com

Solare

2820 Roosevelt Rd., Point Loma, 619-270-9670
solarelounge.com

Cori Pastificio

2977 Upas St., North Park, 619-573-6159
coripasta.com

Catania

7863 Girard Ave., La Jolla, 858-551-5105
cataniasd.com

GO LOCAL
AT THE HILLCREST FARMERS MARKET AND OPEN-AIR BAZAAR

Harboring more small farms than any other county in the nation, San Diego has a bounty of fresh produce year-round, and every day of the week there are several farmers markets to be found where you can sample the produce of regional farmers and treats from local artisans. The Sunday Hillcrest Farmers Market is the largest, drawing more than 10,000 people weekly who peruse the wares of about 175 vendors selling a wide variety of local produce and prepared foods such as bread, cheese, olive oils, and meats. You'll find flowers, clothing, and at one end of the street, the "food court" offers a bounty of international cuisine, from ceviche to African-spiced grilled food, and from Korean barbecue to Vietnamese coffees. In 2026 the market will move back to its original location, but while street reconstruction goes on, the location is around the corner, centered at the 1100 block of University Avenue.

3960 Normal St., Hillcrest, 619-237-1632
hillcrestfarmersmarket.com

TIP

Another good option for a Sunday Farmers Market is La Jolla's, held 9:00 a.m. to 1:00 p.m. at 7335 Girard Avenue (at Genter Street). All proceeds benefit improvements and programs such as art, music, the library, and technology at La Jolla Elementary School: lajollamarket.com

OTHER SAN DIEGO FARMERS MARKETS TO VISIT

Additional information:
sdfarmbureau.org/farmers-market

Escondido (Monday)

3:00 p.m. to 7:00 p.m.
8860 Lawrence Welk Dr.

Coronado (Tuesday)

2:30 p.m. to 6:00 p.m.
1201 First St. (Ferry Landing)

Ocean Beach (Wednesday)

4:00 p.m. to 8:00 p.m.
4900 block of Newport, between Cable and Bacon

North Park (Thursday)

3:00 p.m. to 7:30 p.m.
3000 North Park Way

La Mesa Village (Friday)

3:00 p.m. to 7:00 p.m.
La Mesa Blvd., between 4th St. and Palm Ave.

Little Italy Mercato (Saturday)

8:00 a.m. to 2:00 p.m.
W. Date St. between Kettner Blvd. and Front St.

SURGE TO THE TOP
AT MISTER A'S

The San Diego fine-dining restaurant for more than six decades, Mister A's is my pick as the best sky lounge for sunset—or any time of day, really. A couple other venues are higher, but none quite delivers the wall-to-wall panorama that the dining room and outdoor terrace of Mister A's does. To the east, Balboa Park unfolds just a few hundred feet away; to the south it's a bird's-eye view of the entire downtown cityscape—San Diego Bay curls behind and Coronado Island sits beyond. To the west, Point Loma wraps a protective finger around the bay, while across this scene flies an eye-level procession of jets landing at the airport. Reserve well in advance for a seating just before sunset to indulge in caviar tater tots, king salmon "Wellington," rack of lamb Provençal, or Maine lobster *cacio e pepe*. Take note of less expensive dining alternatives, such as the Saturday Jazz Brunch or the aperitif menu served Sunday through Wednesday evenings. Business casual attire required.

2550 Fifth Ave., 12th Floor, Bankers Hill, 619-239-1377
asrestaurant.com

TIP

Altitude Sky Lounge is a 22nd-floor rooftop alternative, perched atop the Marriott Gaslamp Quarter and looking straight down on the Padres' Petco Park. There's a nightly happy hour (5:00–7:00 p.m.) and deejays spinning on select nights (660 K St., 619-446-6086, altitudeskylounge.com).

22

TOUR THE BAY FOR DINNER

WITH FLAGSHIP CRUISES

A dinner cruise around San Diego Bay reveals this great natural harbor's finest assets: views of the downtown skyline, Coronado Island, Naval Air Station North Island, and of the shipyards along the city's working waterfront. Enjoy the bay in comfort aboard a sunset or nighttime journey with Flagship Cruises, a family-owned operator that has been sailing the bay since 1915. The elegant three-course dinner prepared on-board is served several ways, including a surf and turf dinner with filet mignon and jumbo prawns on Sundays; on weekends try the champagne brunch cruises featuring bottomless mimosas. While not quite gourmet dining, Flagship's seafood is sustainably sourced and most of the produce is local, so tip back a glass of sparkling wine and marvel at the twinkle of city lights as you float beneath the Coronado Bridge.

990 N. Harbor Dr., downtown, 619-234-4111
flagshipsd.com

DEVOUR AN ASIAN FEAST
ON CONVOY STREET

A series of unassuming strip malls tucked between car dealerships along Convoy Street in Kearny Mesa helps cloak a dizzying concentration of Asian cuisines. In this decidedly un-romantic location, a mile from end to end, you could easily spend a couple weeks tasting all the different cultures and foods for lunch and dinner, ranging from Vietnamese to Japanese and from Thai to Chinese, including stops in Hong Kong and Xi'an. Among several dozen eateries, try China Max for soup dumplings and dim sum; YinTang Spicy Hot Pot, where you can build your own steaming bowl of hot pot; or the omakase bar Hidden Fish, which offers an intimate nigiri experience for 13 people at a sitting (reserve early). My favorite: At Shan'xi Magic Kitchen the hearty cuisine of China's Shaanxi province is embraced, including the long, belt-like Biangbiang noodles—try it with spicy cumin lamb. If you're not stuffed silly, visit Sunday Ice Cream, where the mélange of rotating flavors includes black sesame, lychee sorbet, sweet corn, and taro-ube.

Convoy St., between Clairemont Mesa Blvd. and Aero Dr.
Neighborhood: Kearney Mesa

24

TOAST THE LOCAL SUDS
DURING SAN DIEGO BEER WEEK

Serving as a frothy closeout to the long summer, the region's bounteous beer culture is toasted in early November during San Diego Beer Week. The 10-day—who's counting?—county-wide festival is sponsored by the local brewer's guild. The region's craft beers, brewed by more than 150 county breweries, have been collecting serious hardware at competitions around the world. It's a cozy scene—the brewers even collaborate on a Capital of Craft IPA to showcase San Diego's favorite beer style. Today, with craft beer contributing significant annual revenue to the county, Beer Week encompasses more than 500 beer-related events, including food pairing dinners at top restaurants, beer-making classes, meet-the-brewer sessions, and educational sessions. Tasty gluten-free beer, anyone? Chocolate and beer pairings? It's all here, and more.

sdbeer.com/sdbeerweek.html

ELEVATE YOUR BRUNCH GAME
AT MORNING GLORY

Named for a plant with hallucinogenic properties, this over-the-top, brunch-only spot for is known for outrageous, Instagram-worthy décor and breakfast ideas that embrace the globe. That is, once you ascend the stairs and get past the line to get in. Reservations are possible on OpenTable (good luck finding a slot), but don't even bother calling with questions. The room is dominated by a giant, hovering pink neon starburst, underfoot is a pink-and-black tile floor, and handsome windows facing the morning sun are articulated to let in the breeze. The vending machine is stocked with Moët & Chandon, and a tableside cart has makings for Bloody Marys topped with celery foam. The menu hopscotches from Japanese soufflé pancakes to Georgian khachapuri, and from pork belly fried rice to fried chicken and waffles. Brunch at Morning Glory is one cheerful millennial acid trip.

550 W Date St., Little Italy, 619-629-0302
morninggloryb reakfast.com

26

SUCCUMB TO BURGER URGES

AT HODAD'S

As in most American cities, the lowly hamburger has staged an epic revival in San Diego over the last decade. Whether offered on the sly at a gourmet establishment or at the beloved California chain In-N-Out, the options for a tasty burger are endless. Hodad's, an Ocean Beach institution since 1969, offers a classic burger on steroids. Outside, all iterations of beach culture mingle; inside, the décor is surf-sticker chic with car license plates from every state in the Union—plus a motley collection of foreign plates—adorning every square inch of the walls. The "mini" hamburger (available with bacon and/or cheese) is large enough to make a Big Mac go crying for mommy (chicken and veggie options available). The "single" is a monster, as are the thick-cut fries and onion rings. That milk shake? It's served in an overflowing blender, which is why I'll usually opt for michelada (draft beer and spicy bloody Mary mix). O.B. culture doesn't get any grittier—or tastier—than this.

5010 Newport Ave., Ocean Beach, 619-224-4623
945 Broadway, downtown, 619-234-6323
hodadsburgers.com

FIVE MORE BURGER JOINTS WORTH BITING INTO

Crazee Burger

3993 30th St., North Park, 619-282-6044
crazeeburger.com

Starlight

3175 India St., Midtown, 619-618-2830
www.starlitesd.com

Rocky's Crown Pub

3786 Ingraham St., Pacific Beach, 858-273-9140
rockyburgers.com

Public House La Jolla

830 Kline St., La Jolla, 858-551-9210
the-publichouse.com

Tanner's Prime Burger

510 Vista Way, Oceanside
tannersprimeburgers.com

27

LIVE OUT YOUR POLYNESIAN FANTASIES

WITH A BALI HAI MAI TAI

Family owned and operated since 1954, Bali Hai is renowned for San Diego's most iconic cocktail, the Mai Tai—about 2.9 million have been sold to date. The popular restaurant boasts that their recipe for the tropical concoction is fruit-free. Instead, bartenders mix Coruba Jamaican Dark Rum, Ron Castillo Light Rum, a dash of orange liqueur, a dash of Trader Vic's orgeat syrup, and a splash of sweet and sour, delivering an oversized and powerfully potent potion. For garnish, this expansive tiki temple offers a sweeping panorama of San Diego Bay and the downtown skyline, stirred with hand-carved sculptures, tapa cloths, and other Polynesian artifacts. The venue serves up such South Pacific delicacies as coconut shrimp, Hawaiian tuna poke, and lobster wonton tacos, along with a fleet of surf-and-turf favorites.

2230 Shelter Island Dr., Shelter Island, 619-222-1181
balihairestaurant.com

28

FORAGE FOR GLOBAL FOODS
AT LIBERTY PUBLIC MARKET

Who would have thought a decade ago that Liberty Station, the former Naval Training Center, would become one of San Diego's favorite places to hang? In addition to restaurants, a movie theater, arts district, and even an outdoor ice-skating rink at New Year's, inside the former mess hall and commissary is the biggest draw, Liberty Public Market. More than 35 vendors offer a range of cuisines from quick-service counters. Try Bao Bar for Chinese buns and boba tea, or at Latin Chef look for Peruvian ceviche and beef heart kebabs, or step up to Olala, where savory and sweet crepes are prepared using organic buckwheat flour imported from Brittany. There's also fresh artisan pastas, Hungarian chimney cakes, a bottle shop, occasional live acts, and much more.

2820 Historic Decatur Rd., Point Loma, 619-487-9346
libertypublicmarketsd.com

29

REEL IN FISH TACOS FOR LUNCH

AT RUBIO'S

Without a doubt, San Diego's one indispensable fast food is the humble fish taco. Credit a local surfer, Ralph Rubio, for the "research" he put into tasting fish tacos out of thatch-roof beach shacks in Baja. The recipe he brought home and popularized was batter-dipped, deep-fried fish (now Alaskan pollock) folded in corn tortillas and garnished with shredded cabbage, salsa, and tangy *crema* as a sauce. Born in 1983, the tacos caught on, and today you'll find Rubio's Coastal Grill in about a hundred locations throughout Southern California. Menus at the fast-casual restaurants have expanded to include other Mexican dishes, and beer and wine are served, but with 270 million sold to date, need I tell you what the most popular item is? No doubt, honoring Taco Tuesday deals helps nudge those numbers along.

4504 E Mission Bay Dr., Pacific Beach, 858-272-2801
Other locations throughout San Diego
rubios.com

TIP

So ubiquitous is the fish taco to San Diego that it's a staple on many restaurant menus. For a gourmet take with a dreamy rooftop view, head to George's Ocean Terrace, where the tacos are made with grilled cod and topped with green papaya slaw, mango-habanero salsa, cilantro, and crema.

1250 Prospect St., La Jolla, 858-454-4244
georgesatthecove.com

30

CROSS THE BORDER
TO DISCOVER MEXICO'S PREMIERE WINE REGION

While California wineries are treasured for their quality and abundance, it was Mexico that produced the first wine in the Americas, using grapevines brought over by the Spanish in the 16th century. The humid winters and dry, warm summers of Northern Baja allow for most of the same varietals produced in California, and Valle de Guadalupe, located northeast of Ensenada, is just 90 minutes from the San Diego–Tijuana border. Here, wines of surprising quality and finesse can be enjoyed—they're rarely exported north of the border. While driving down to Guadalupe Valley isn't hard, after considering insurance, border ministrations, and designated drivers, you may want to leave the driving to someone else. Baja Winery Tours offers 10-hour private and group tours. You'll visit three different wineries for eye-opening tastings and enjoy a three-course gourmet lunch at a fine restaurant. Passport required.

Baja Winery Tours
619-535-9994
bajawinerytours.com

TIP

Temecula is one of Southern California's major wine-producing regions and is located just an hour north of San Diego. There are more than 45 wineries in Temecula Wine Country, and many have tasting rooms and restaurants as well as some gift shops.

temeculawines.org

Museums of Balboa Park

MUSIC AND ENTERTAINMENT

31

DECLARE INDEPENDENCE
WITH THE BIG BAY BOOM

Coronado, home to a sizeable contingent of military veterans, throws one of the most popular Independence Day celebrations in the nation. The first parade was held in 1888, and it's become an annual tradition since the 1940s. Today, upward of a half-million people attend, and residents and visitors alike start lining the Orange Avenue parade route before dawn. The first activity is a 12K run at 7:00 a.m., followed by a Rough Water Swim event. The parade starts at 10:00 a.m., with a patriotic naval presence in the floats and bands; for the rest of the day an art show and concert fill out Spreckels Park. While there are fireworks at Coronado's Glorietta Bay, the big show is hosted by San Diego, where one of the nation's largest fireworks displays—dubbed the Big Bay Boom—blooms.

1100 Orange Ave., Coronado and San Diego Bay, 866-599-7242
coronado.ca.us

TIP

The Big Bay Boom is launched simultaneously from four barges around North San Diego Bay. The show can be seen from Shelter Island, Harbor Island, the Embarcadero, Marina District, Seaport Village, and Coronado Ferry Landing.

32

GROOVE TO LIVE JAMS
AT THE BELLY UP

Occupying a funky Quonset hut in Solana Beach, since 1974 the Belly Up has hosted critically acclaimed and international artists of all genres for more than 45 years. On any given night the live music ranges from Tom Jones to 10,000 Maniacs and from Death Cab for Cutie to Rufus Wainwright—plus up-and-coming artists showcasing alternative rock, reggae, jazz, Latin, and more. Even the Rolling Stones took the stage here in 2015 for an unadvertised concert. Most shows at the 600-capacity venue are standing room only—intimate yet comfortable, catering to regulars with inoffensive drink prices. For those who want to dodge the 30-minute drive from downtown, the Coaster commuter rail stop is just two blocks away, and the adjacent Tavern serves a fusion of California and Mediterranean flavors before and after the show. Advance tickets recommended, available through the website and at the box office.

143 S Cedros Ave., Solana Beach, 858-481-8140
bellyup.com

LISTEN UP FOR SUMMER POPS
AT THE SAN DIEGO SYMPHONY'S SHELL

Long a fixture of the summer outdoor music scene, the San Diego Symphony debuted a permanent outdoor concert venue in 2020. The Rady Shell is the only such waterfront facility on the West Coast. Trimmed by the lights of downtown, the Shell provides sophisticated acoustics in a park-like setting next to San Diego Bay. Summer "pops" concerts by the acclaimed San Diego Symphony cover a range of genres—from classical to Broadway, Jazz, and R&B. On some nights, movies from such series as *Harry Potter* or *Star Wars* are presented with live orchestral accompaniment; on others, tributes to musical treasures like The Beatles or Miles Davis are featured. Meals are available at the Plaza Dining Pavilion, or you can arrange for a designer picnic by prominent local chefs (place orders by 4 p.m. the day prior). Jacobs Music Center, also downtown, hosts the orchestra's regular season, from October through May.

206 Marina Park Way, downtown, 619-235-0804
sandiegosymphony.org

TIP

Any time of year, bring a sweater to San Diego for cool bayside nights and outdoor dining.

34

SEEK YOUR FORTUNE IN SAN DIEGO'S BACKCOUNTRY

AT A CASINO RESORT

With the largest concentration of Native American tribes of any county in the United States—18 in all—San Diego's backcountry has an array of bustling casino resorts. The first of the casinos was built by the Sycuan people, a simple bingo palace that opened in 1983. In 2019, the Sycuan Band completed a $260 million project to create a Las Vegas–style casino hotel and resort. In addition to 302 hotel rooms in a 12-story tower, the expansion includes a spa and fitness center, a cabana-lined pool and lazy river, and an enlarged gaming floor with 2,300 slot machines and 54 table games. Nonsmokers can enjoy slots and table games and other amenities in a new, smoke-free environment. A complimentary shuttle accesses the 45-hole Singing Hills Golf Club, three miles away.

5469 Casino Way, Harbison Canyon, 619-445-6002
sycuan.com

PURR WITH THE FELINES OF SAN DIEGO ZOO

More than 12,000 creatures representing 680 species reside at this celebrated and influential zoo, the world's most visited. Occupying a lush, 100-acre nook within Balboa Park, it offers more than enough to fill an animal lover's entire day. One spectacular section, Africa Rocks, transforms a canyon into habitats that spotlight Africa's biodiversity, ranging from penguins to leopards, and from meerkats to baboons. In 2024, a pair of giant pandas were welcomed back to the zoo in a reimagined habitat four times larger than the previous panda enclosure. Smart visitors embark on one of several specialty tours offered on select days, such as Crazy About Cats, a two-hour exploration behind the scenes to visit some of the most iconic cat species. Private visits feature a rotating list of marquee stars including jaguars, lions, tigers, mountain lions, fishing cats, leopards, ocelots, or servals (reserve in advance).

2920 Zoo Dr., Balboa Park, 619-231-1515
sandiegozoo.com

FIVE MORE REASONS THE SAN DIEGO ZOO IS NOT JUST ANY ZOO

San Diego Zoo founder Dr. Harry Wegeforth brought home plants from every location animals were acquired, ensuring a naturalistic environment. With more than 700,000 plants, the flora from a variety of climate zones are said to be worth more than the animal collection.

The zoo was at the forefront of the move toward "cageless" environments, using moats to separate animals from humans, rather than wire or fences. Some of the largest free-flight aviaries anywhere are here, allowing us to enter the giant cage to observe colorful birds in close proximity in a naturalistic setting.

Many species are seen almost nowhere else. In 2015 only 60 Amur leopards were thought to exist in the wild in Russia and Northern China—a pair lives here. The strange platypus, an egg-laying mammal, is found nowhere outside Australia, except the zoo's Safari Park.

The zoo is involved with animal preservation in 45 countries around the world and has engineered many "firsts" in breeding—from the nearly-extinct California condor to recently discovered Visayan warty pigs—and more than 180 rhinos have been born at the zoo's Safari Park.

Beyond fast-food options, Albert's Restaurant is like a treehouse oasis. Offering sit-down dining and a full bar, it's a great place in which to break up the middle of the day, when animals are laziest (reservations advised).

ROAR AND SNORE WITH THE BEASTIES

AT SAN DIEGO ZOO SAFARI PARK

The African safari is a bucket-list journey for most of us, but at the San Diego Zoo Safari Park you can sleep in a tent, in close proximity to giraffes, rhinos, and antelope. After checking in for Roar and Snore, you'll take an after-hours guided walk to observe the animals' nocturnal life. Following dinner, campfire tales and s'mores are punctuated by calls emanating from dark corners of the park. Enjoy a pancake breakfast in the morning, and take the day to see the rest of the park. The 1,800-acre Safari Park is located 33 miles north of downtown and is well worth visiting even if you don't spend the night. More than 3,100 animals live in the naturalistic settings, with sprawling enclosures replicating such environments as African forests and Australian grasslands, shared by multiple species interacting much as they would in the wild.

15500 San Pasqual Valley Rd., Escondido, 760-747-8702
Neighborhood: San Pasqual Valley
sdzsafaripark.org

TIP

The cloudiest months of the year in San Diego come at the end of spring, lasting into early summer. If you explore San Diego during this period you can look forward to hearing the local excuses, "May Gray" and "June Gloom." One option: Head away from the coast, where the marine layer lingers longest. The Safari Park, located about 16 miles inland, is usually sunny and warm for most of the day during our grayest months.

DROP A NEEDLE
AT PART TIME LOVER

Vinyl bars are a requisite component of the world's coolest cities. San Diego doesn't miss a beat here with this partnership between Folk Arts Records, one of the city's long-standing repositories of rare vinyl, and local restaurant and bar entrepreneur Consortium Holdings. They've upcycled a former dive bar and infused it with Art Deco and Prairie School aesthetics, even calling on the Frank Lloyd Wright Foundation to design the bar and its table lamps. If the nightclub feels like a time warp into the mid-century Midwest, that may be the idea, and it's paired with a deep affection for music, especially the powerful hi-fi sound of analog recordings, which boast a warmer sound and wider range of frequencies than digitally captured recordings. The communal listening experience ranges from acid jazz to blues, funk, and tropicália, and guest deejays spin nightly, including touring musicians and pros like KCRW's Chris Douridas. The Japanese-inspired cocktail list covers all the bases, and the record shop in back stays open late.

3829 30th St., North Park, 619-932-4434
parttimeloverhifi.com

CELEBRATE CHRISTMAS
AT THE SAN DIEGO PARADE OF LIGHTS

In mid-December, for two consecutive Sundays, San Diego Bay is lit up like a Christmas tree during the San Diego Parade of Lights. Cheered on by 100,000 spectators, dozens of boats of all shapes and sizes follow a parade route beginning at Shelter Island and passing Harbor Island, the Embarcadero, Seaport Village, and Ferry Landing in Coronado. This tradition, which celebrates its 55th anniversary in 2025, has become synonymous with the holiday season in San Diego, with all manner of private vessels participating, decorated to the gills. Judges score each boat based on lighting, music, special effects, and originality, with prizes that are worth the effort. While it's fun to experience the show on the water, for landlubbers there are lots of great locations along the route, including many restaurants along Harbor Island, the Embarcadero and in Coronado.

1220 Rosecrans St., Ste. 414, 619-224-2240
Neighborhoods: Downtown, Point Loma, Coronado
sdparadeoflights.org

39

FLIRT WITH SEADRAGONS AND SEAHORSES
AT BIRCH AQUARIUM

Killer whales? Been there. Elephants? Done that. Sometimes it's the most demure critters that pack the biggest wallop, and the Seadragons & Seahorses exhibit at the Birch Aquarium will have you swooning with delight. The seadragons and seahorses cavort in a giant tank, while a behind-the-scenes tour immerses guests in the facility's ongoing, 30-year seahorse research program. Birch, the public side of the world-renowned Scripps Institution of Oceanography, is the leader in seahorse and seadragon breeding conservation, but there's much more to see. With around 60 habitats representing various Pacific Ocean environments such as tide pools, a coral garden, and a giant kelp forest, creatures on display range from fierce tiger sharks to garibaldi (California's State Marine Fish), and from fanciful white anemones to voluptuous moon jellies. There are also absorbing interpretive exhibits on cutting-edge research at Scripps.

2300 Expedition Way, 858-534-3474
aquarium.ucsd.edu

TIP

Each summer in July, the aquarium's little blue penguins go through what's called a catastrophic molt—that is, a makeover—as the penguins shed old feathers to be replaced by new ones. For a few weeks the little birds look adorably fluffy and punk.

40

HULA FOR YOUR DINNER
AT SUNSET LUAUS ON THE BAY

If a vacation to Hawaii isn't in the cards this year, maybe a trip to the Catamaran Resort in Pacific Beach will work a little island magic. Every summer from mid-June through August, a weekly Sunset Luau on the Bay is held on Thursday evenings along the placid shores of Mission Bay. The family-friendly luau includes an all-you-can-eat buffet featuring scrumptious roast Kalua pig and live entertainment by the local group Pride of Polynesia. Hula with the best of them, drum along with the performers, but stand back for the torch dancers when they take the stage. The meal also includes such tropical delights as Hawaiian sweet rolls, lomi-lomi salmon salad, macadamia-nut-crusted mahi, and pineapple fried rice. Bring a sweater for those unexpectedly cool summer evenings.

3999 Mission Blvd., Pacific Beach, 858-488-1081
catamaranresort.com/sunset-luaus

41

PADDLE UP FOR TOP TOURING ACTS
AT HUMPHREY'S CONCERTS BY THE BAY

Beloved by San Diegans and visiting performers alike, Humphrey's is a 1,400-seat outdoor venue sandwiched between bobbing yachts in a Shelter Island marina and a Polynesian-themed hotel. The unique ambiance leads performers to return again and again—Ray Charles is said to have performed at Humphrey's 37 times. The acts run the gamut, from Ringo Starr to Bill Maher, and from John Legend to Bob Dylan, attracting multiple generations of attendees since its opening in 1982. The annual season runs from May through September, though a few acts sneak in just before and after. Tickets are sold at the box office and through Ticketmaster, but note that the best seats—the first eight or so rows—are usually reserved for those buying a dinner-and-show package with the adjacent restaurant, also called Humphrey's.

2241 Shelter Island Drive, Point Loma, 619-224-3577
humphreysconcerts.com

TIP

Humphrey's features prominently in the moving, Oscar-winning 2013 documentary, *20 Feet from Stardom.*

KID AROUND
AT LEGOLAND

The world's most famous plastic building blocks get their due at Legoland California, nirvana for most eight-year-olds (and for a few adults who still cherish their Lego days). Beautifully landscaped with bonsai trees, the 128-acre park is chock-full of gentle rides and pint-sized roller coasters, with world landmarks recreated from Legos, a miniature golf course, and Dino Valley, offering three rides, an interactive play area, and costume characters. In 2026, a new attraction will launch: a space-themed land featuring a family-friendly immersive indoor roller coaster that will zoom through an uncharted galaxy, blasting off from the Legoland Spaceport 866 launchpad. In all, 60 million Lego bricks were used to create this whimsical fantasyland. There's a water park for splashy fun, and the Sea Life Aquarium—with real, not plastic, fish—is right next door (separate admission required). While some teens may find Legoland a bit of a snooze, it's perfect for kids ages two to 12.

1 Legoland Dr., Carlsbad, 760-918-5346
legoland.com/california

TIP

When Legoland opens, many visitors hop in line for the first rides encountered (neither of which are special)—it's better to head to the back side of the park where lines are shorter for the first hour or so.

MEET A "SEA CANARY" AT SEAWORLD

Although the SeaWorld theme park empire got its start in San Diego in 1964, in later years as the parks multiplied, the marine focus has taken a back seat to roller coasters. But peel back the thrill ride veneer and you'll find solid animal encounters, including a few that go beyond pirouetting dolphins and fluke flinging killer whales. In-water interactions with the affable beluga whales inside their watery habitat are one example. Guests wearing wetsuits are allowed to touch and feed these sociable white whales. Nicknamed "sea canaries" for their cheerful calls, belugas are listed as threatened or endangered in the Arctic, their natural environment. Afterward, check out the park's 500 other species, including the only emperor penguin colony in the western hemisphere, and Shark Reef, home to sand tiger, bonnethead, blacktip, and whitetip reef sharks.

500 SeaWorld Dr., Mission Bay, 619-222-4732
seaworldsandiego.com

ROCK
AT THE CASBAH

San Diego's most iconic location for indie rock, this intimate venue on the edge of Little Italy has been a launching pad for local and national talent since 1989, hosting such legends as Nirvana, Arcade Fire, the White Stripes, and Smashing Pumpkins before they hit it big. Don't look for such names today—the Casbah has a capacity of just 200—but because the management books much bigger stages around town, such as the Observatory, you should still come here for authentic discoveries in an unfiltered dive bar environment. Drinks are cheap, they have a back room with pool tables and pinball, and there's an outdoor patio where you can enjoy the stars between acts. Lines are long nearly every night for up-and-coming touring acts as well as the more popular local groups—get onto the mailing list to access tickets as soon as they're released.

2501 Kettner Blvd., Little Italy, 619-232-4355
casbahmusic.com

45

LOWER YOUR STANDARDS FOR THE ADULT ANTICS OF OVER-THE-LINE

Sure, San Diego may not have a professional football team to cheer, but the city can still point to over-the-line as the sporting event at which its residents excel. An informal novelty game started by members of the Old Mission Beach Athletic Club in the 1950s, the annual tournament gathers 1,200 or more teams for two weekends of bawdy revelry in mid-July. Similar to baseball, three-person over-the-line teams include a batter, pitcher, and a fielder; the court is any available patch of sand on Fiesta Island, in Mission Bay. The annual tournament divides teams by gender and age (some players are well into their 80s). Beer is involved (no glass, please), there's a lot of skin in this game, and team names sometimes swing toward the wildly inappropriate—mostly unprintable here (which is why minors are discouraged).

Fiesta Island, Mission Bay
ombac.org/over-the-line

SAIL AWAY TO DISTANT HORIZONS
FROM THE PORT OF SAN DIEGO

It takes a lot to lure locals away from San Diego, but cruise lines tempt us with more than a hundred sailings to far-flung ports annually. Dominating the field is Holland America Line, which offers a wealth of seven-night roundtrips fall through spring to the Mexican Riviera (Cabo San Lucas, Mazatlán, Puerto Vallarta), along with longer roundtrip voyages to Hawaii and one-way itineraries to the Caribbean and Florida via the Panama Canal. The *Disney Magic* and *Disney Wonder* sail out of San Diego on journeys ranging three to seven nights, fall through spring, to Mexico, Catalina Island, and through the Panama Canal. Norwegian and Royal Caribbean also offer three-, four-, and seven-night itineraries to the Mexican Riviera fall through spring. Come April, many cruise lines reposition these ships for the Alaskan season, resulting in bargains on one-way cruises from San Diego to Seattle or Vancouver. In October, the trip is offered in reverse.

1140 N. Harbor Dr., downtown, 619-400-4744
portofsandiego.org/experiences/plan-your-cruise

WANDER THROUGH THE FLOWER FIELDS
OF CARLSBAD

Carlsbad and neighboring Encinitas represent a noteworthy commercial flower-growing region, and each spring a beguiling panoply of color can be seen at the Flower Fields, a hillside setting that has served as home to a spectacular flower display since the 1950s. Growers from Carlsbad Ranch spend months preparing the fields with a meticulously planned palette, filling 50 acres with thousands of Giant Tecolote Ranunculus flowers. A member of the buttercup family, the flower remains in bloom for up to 10 weeks, from early March to mid-May. A quarter-million visitors flock to the fields each year, to walk amid the vibrant landscape, and there are also rose and theme gardens, fresh strawberries, a cymbidium greenhouse, a poinsettia display, a sweet pea maze, and antique tractor wagon rides. Picnicking is allowed, and shopping at Carlsbad Premium Outlets is nearby.

5704 Paseo Del Norte, Carlsbad, 760-431-0352
theflowerfields.com

48

TAKE ME OUT TO A PADRES GAME
AT PETCO PARK

The San Diego Padres' home field is one of the most thoughtfully designed, aesthetically pleasing Major League ballparks—a retro classic planted right in the center of bustling downtown. How many other teams have a left field foul pole at the corner of a 116-year-old building? The brick walls of the four-story Western Metal Supply Co. warehouse serve as a prominent fixture, along with six other historic buildings. None of this impedes great sightlines, coupled with views of the city skyline, the bay, and Balboa Park. And while 40,000-seat Petco Park isn't the first to offer sushi alongside franks and fries, you'll find authentic Neapolitan pizza out of a brick oven, a barbecue stand run by former Padres pitcher Randy Jones, and mouth-watering carnitas tacos—plus the best lineup of craft beers in the majors. Check out the Park in the Park (aka Gallagher Square), a grassy slope behind the outfield offering bargain admission. BYO blanket and cushions (no hard-frame chairs allowed).

100 Park Blvd., downtown, 619-795-5000
mlb.com/padres

TIP

Parking at Petco is costly. Consider taking the trolley, which has three stops a short walk from the park entrances.

Torrey Pines Gilderport

SPORTS AND RECREATION

49

RIDE THE MISSION BEACH BOARDWALK

Okay, so it's not a real boardwalk. Still, the concrete walkway running parallel to the shoreline from Pacific Beach to Mission Beach is a great place to walk, jog, skate, rollerblade, cycle, and people-watch through one of San Diego's most iconic scenes. I like biking it, navigating the steady procession of road hazards—dogs, strollers, surfboards—with the sun high overhead. The boardwalk can be crowded, especially on summer weekends, so plan on riding slowly. But that lazy, meandering pace means you'll soak up a lot of the cheery beach vibe, including a plethora of tattoos, piercings, and bronzed skin. There are a number of beach bars to stop at for liquid refreshment along the way. Bike rental shops are found from one end of Mission Boulevard to the other, but parking is easiest in the lots near Belmont Park.

Pacific Beach, Mission Beach

TIP

Mission Beach is a slender isthmus just a few blocks wide. There is another path on the side closest to Mission Bay, Bayside Lane, and it is less crowded and easier for children and budding cyclists.

BAG FIVE PEAKS
AT MISSION TRAILS REGIONAL PARK

Whether you stroll, pedal, or climb it, 8,000-acre Mission Trails Regional Park, the sixth-largest municipally-owned park in the US, is a place to escape the freeway rat race, reconnect with San Diego's native landscapes, and more. This beautiful recreational area inside the city (12 miles from downtown) encompasses rugged hills, a splendid canyon, and the slender San Diego River. There are 60-plus miles of trails and five peaks, including 1,592-foot Cowles Mountain, the highest point in the city. You'll get fine views from the top, a five-mile roundtrip hike from Big Rock—but why stop there? Park rangers encourage residents and visitors alike to ascend all five peaks, whether in a day (11.5 miles) or over separate visits. The visitor center is worth checking out, with state-of-the-art exhibits, souvenirs, and ranger-led walks several times weekly.

1 Father Junipero Serra Trail, Mission Gorge, 619-668-3281
mtrp.org

51

MAKE A DATE WITH CETACEANS

ON A WHALE-WATCHING TOUR

Starting in early December each year, 20,000 gray whales migrate between the summer feeding grounds of Alaska to the calm calving lagoons of Baja California, passing close to San Diego. From February through April, they head back north on their 6,000-mile journey with calves in tow. A number of companies offer whale-watching tours, but for a more intimate experience climb aboard Next Level Sailing's yacht, *America*, a replica of a 139-foot sailboat built in 1850 that some call the world's most famous racing yacht. Gray whales 40 to 50 feet long are the focus in winter, and you'll see these gentle creatures swimming gracefully and resolutely through the ocean. Humpbacks arrive in March, and minke whales in summer. In recent years blue whales—typically found in deep waters—have begun feeding on krill along the coast in summer. Lucky summer visitors may witness earth's largest creature, a behemoth weighing up to 300,000 pounds, and even occasional killer whales.

2050 Shelter Island Dr., Shelter Island, 619-577-4008
nextlevelsailing.com

LEAP INTO THE VOID
AT TORREY PINES GLIDERPORT

San Diego's aviation history is robust: From the *Spirit of St. Louis*, built here in 1927, to the US Navy's Topgun training established at Naval Station Miramar, the region is full of firsts. Accordingly, seafront Torrey Pines Gliderport—where Charles Lindbergh made his maiden flight—is a great place for novices to take a first, thrilling paraglide flight, especially when winds are at their gusty best, from March through June. You'll strap into a bucket seat in front of an experienced pilot, inch toward the edge of bluffs that drop 372 feet to the tawny sands of Black's Beach, and as wind fills the elliptical wing, you'll soar heavenward. The tandem flight ($200) involves figure-eight loops along the edge of the cliff for about 30 minutes, resulting in a ride that's more deeply rewarding than any theme park roller coaster.

2800 Torrey Pines Scenic Dr., Torrey Pines, 858-452-9858
flytorrey.com

TIP

If the idea of stepping off the edge of a cliff puts you in a sweat, ogle the scene at the Cliffhanger Café and watch aviators leap into the void.

TEE OFF AT AMERICA'S FINEST GOLF COURSES AT TORREY PINES

The municipal Torrey Pines Golf Course sits adjacent to a state preserve on bluffs overlooking the sparkling Pacific Ocean—one of world's most picturesque golf settings. The 36-hole paradise was built in 1957, and for more than 50 years it has been included in the PGA Tour. In 2008 Torrey Pines hosted one of the most dramatic US Opens in the history of the tournament, when Tiger Woods defeated Rocco Mediate during a sudden death playoff (the US Open was back here in 2021). While the North Course is spectacular, the South Course is more challenging, and has more sea-facing play. Although the course is open to the public, securing a tee time is tough. Reservations within seven days or fewer are available to residents only, but it's worth the effort. The facilities include a driving range, practice putting greens, and one of the largest golf shops in the western US.

11480 N Torrey Pines Rd., Torrey Pines, 877-581-7171
sandiego.gov/park-and-recreation/golf/torreypines

MORE FINE SAN DIEGO COURSES

The Crossings at Carlsbad

5800 The Crossings Dr., Carlsbad, 760-444-1800
thecrossingsatcarlsbad.com

Coronado Municipal Golf Course

2000 Visalia Row, Coronado, 619-522-2455
golfcoronado.com

The Grand Golf Club at Fairmont Grand Del Mar

5300 Grand Del Mar Way, Del Mar
858-314-1930
fairmont.com/san-diego

Balboa Park Golf Course

2600 Golf Course Dr., South Park, 619-235-1184
sandiego.gov/park-and-recreation/golf/bpgolf

Encinitas Ranch Golf Course

1275 Quail Gardens Dr., Encinitas, 760-944-1936
encinitasranchgolf.com

FROLIC WITH ROVER

AT DOG BEACH, PAMPER HIM AT THE DOG WASH

When dogs dream of heaven, the scene probably looks a bit like Dog Beach, a stretch of sand at the north end of Ocean Beach that was designated in 1972 as one of the nation's first official leash-free beaches. Once paws hit the sand, the leashes come off and the running, splashing, fetching, posing, and socializing begins. Water fountains, doggie bags, and even tennis balls and toys are available. In short, Dog Beach is a joy for canines—a melting pot for dogs of all sizes, shapes, colors, creeds, and breeds. Most of the nearby bars and restaurants are dog-friendly, but after playing you'll probably want a bath for Rover, so head first to nearby Dog Beach Dog Wash (4933 Voltaire St., 619-523-1700) where you'll find specialty shampoos along with grooming and nail trimming services.

5156 W Point Loma Blvd., Ocean Beach, 619-221-8899
dogbeachsd.com

STRIP TO YOUR BIRTHDAY SUIT
AT BLACK'S BEACH

On San Diego's curious roster of firsts is the nation's earliest public clothing-optional beach. While the era of legal nude sunbathing at Black's Beach lasted only a few years during the mid-1970s, the character of this secluded and beautiful shoreline was firmly established. What has kept Black's special is the difficulty of reaching this two-mile-long stretch of sand. You'll either clamber down one of two poorly maintained trails descending the 300-foot bluffs on either side of the Torrey Pines Gliderport—one steep, the other steeper—or you need to meander more than a mile along the shoreline from the closest road access points on either end (one at the La Jolla Shores, the other at the Torrey Pines State Beach parking lot). Note that there are no facilities and lifeguards are scarce, but citations for nudity are rare.

12000 block of N Torrey Pines Rd., Torrey Pines

SKATE BY THE SEA FOR CHRISTMAS AT THE HOTEL DEL CORONADO

Who says it's 72 degrees year-round in San Diego? Each December, the historic Hotel del Coronado transforms into a lavish holiday wonderland featuring beautiful decorations, including a giant Christmas tree in the main lobby and thousands of white lights adorning the historic Victorian building and grounds. With activities scheduled for guests of all ages, the most uniquely Southern California experience is the Del's Skating by the Sea, featuring beachfront ice-skating, with the Pacific Ocean tossing nearby. The scene is created by converting the oceanfront Windsor Lawn—wedding central for most of the year—into a beloved ice rink, starting the week prior to Thanksgiving and running through New Year's Day. The skating is a splurge (reservations recommended), but watching is free, and the event comes complete with fire pits, holiday music, and drinks to warm you up.

1500 Orange Ave., Coronado, 619-522-8100
hoteldel.com

TRACK DOWN A DEEP-FRIED TWINKIE AT THE SAN DIEGO COUNTY FAIR

Drawing more than 1.5 million attendees annually, San Diego's county fair is the largest in the US. The month-long event, held at the Del Mar Fairgrounds and traditionally ending on the Fourth of July, began in 1880 as a way to bring local farmers together to share ideas, hold competitions for the best pies and produce, and host horseback beauty pageants to a chalk art invitational. While the fair continues to celebrate agriculture and community pride, it has grown into a multifaceted entertainment mecca featuring animal and farm exhibits, local and nationally recognized musical performers, retail and hobby tents, carnival rides, and the most calorie-packed food choices imaginable. You'll want to set aside an entire day and evening for your visit to cover all the fair has to offer, and be prepared for traffic snarls going and returning home, especially on weekends.

2260 Jimmy Durante Blvd., Del Mar, 858-755-1161
sdfair.com

58

KAYAK WITH WHALES AND SEA LIONS AND SHARKS, OH MY!

San Diego's number one adventure tour suitable for all ages is kayaking through the La Jolla Ecological Reserve to La Jolla's sea caves. No previous kayak experience is necessary; you'll enjoy sea lions sunbathing on the rocks from up close, and you'll see the California state fish, the bright orange Garibaldi, swimming under your kayak near La Jolla Cove. With Everyday California you'll paddle from La Jolla Shores into one of the seven sea caves (conditions permitting), and then "surf" your kayak back to the beach. Then, during summer months you'll encounter one of the world's largest schools of leopard sharks congregating in wading-depth water. The four-to-five-foot sharks are harmless to humans, but you may find yourself swimming with dozens of the docile creatures. Alternately, in winter months Everyday California takes kayakers two miles offshore to observe gray whales on their annual migration from Alaska to Baja California.

2261 Avenida de la Playa, La Jolla Shores, 858-454-6195
everydaycalifornia.com

BITE OFF POTATO CHIP ROCK ON A HIKE TO MT. WOODSON

High atop Mount Woodson is a tasty natural rock formation that has become an Instagram icon. Aptly named Potato Chip Rock, the wafer-thin granite formation protrudes from just below the summit and into a sweeping view of Poway and the Blue Sky Ecological Preserve. Along the way are lots of cracks and bouldering challenges for climbers to tackle. The exposed hike from the Lake Poway trailhead involves a 7.6-mile round trip and an elevation gain exceeding 2,000 feet, so the ascent is not for sissies. In summer, the ranger station reports regular heat stroke rescues from hikers who aren't carrying the recommended two liters of water per person. But the journey is worth the time, and you'll come home having taken advantage of an unusual photo op of a social media icon to share with your friends.

Trailhead: 14644 Lake Poway Rd., Poway, 858-668-4772
poway.org/DocumentCenter/View/8013/Poway-Trails-Guide-and-Map-2020

TIP

A shorter route to the summit takes the Mt. Woodson Road, closed to private vehicles, which leads up the east flank of the mountain from Highway 67.

60

EASE ALONG SUNSET CLIFFS

FOR DREAMY SEASIDE VISTAS

San Diego's loveliest sunset stroll is along the edge of aptly named Sunset Cliffs, the rugged coastline that bridges the Ocean Beach and Point Loma neighborhoods. Perfect for families with kids, snuggling lovers, or solo types looking for a backdrop for introspection, the path follows Sunset Cliffs Boulevard as it winds south along the wave-sculpted cliffs for 1.5 miles. Start from the Inn at Sunset Cliffs—parking along the road is usually available just beyond the Inn. Surfers often ply the gnarly waves, and the inland side is fronted by one beautiful—often historic—house after another. There's a 68-acre park at Ladera Street, where you'll find arches and sea caves. Don't wander close to the cliff edge; the slowly eroding bluffs have claimed many lives over the decades.

Sunset Cliffs Boulevard Ocean Beach, Ocean Beach
sandiego.gov/park-and-recreation/parks/regional/shoreline/sunset

TIP

Another fine coastline worth exploring is the bluffs below downtown La Jolla. Start from the intersection of Prospect Street and Coast Boulevard and follow the wave-worn sandstone south to La Jolla Tidepools, about 1.2 miles in all.

MUSS YOUR HAIR AND RATTLE YOUR BONES
ON THE GIANT DIPPER

Built in 1925, during the golden age of wooden roller coasters, the Giant Dipper at Belmont Park is a vintage seafront coaster that still packs a thrill (though hopefully not when you get the chiropractor's bill!). First opened on July 4, 1925, the park's zenith was in the early 1930s, when riders paid just 15 cents to roll along the dips and turns. Although the park fell on hard times over ensuing decades, in 1990 the coaster was restored at a cost of $2 million and declared a National Historic Landmark. Special day passes are available encompassing many of Belmont Park's other attractions, including carnival-style rides, a climbing wall, a zip line, arcades, go-carts, bumper cars, an 18-hole miniature golf course, and a three-level laser tag arena. Belmont Park is ideal for families, friends, and parties for any occasion.

3146 Mission Blvd., Mission Beach, 858-488-1549
belmontpark.com

MASTER THE WAVES
WITH A SURF DIVA

You probably know that San Diego is home to some of the best waves on the West Coast. If you're already comfortable on a board, you'll find popular breaks at Tourmaline Surf Park in Pacific Beach, at Windansea, and along the Silver Strand. Many area surf shops rent gear, and the best waves land August through November. La Jolla Shores has gentler waves, and this is where world famous Surf Diva Surf School offers private and group lessons for all ages, allowing anyone to learn how to surf through lessons by professional instructors. It's the largest school on the West Coast, and the expert surf instructors place a special emphasis on teaching women and girls (although men are, of course, welcome, too!). Teenage divas and devos will delight in the shop's boutique, stocked with beach fashions including Surf Diva's own line of swim and active wear. Board rentals also available.

2160 Avenida de la Playa, La Jolla Shores, 858-454-8273
surfdiva.com

RUN WITH
THE GRUNIONS

No, this is not some new marathon, nor a creature from Seussland. Grunions are a slippery little fish unique to Southern California and Northern Baja, and for a few months each year their odd nighttime mating ritual provides a delightful show—to those in the know. On select nights, the slender, silvery fish ride waves onto the wet beach, where they writhe and wriggle, burrowing and spawning before returning to the sea. The runs happen only March through August, a couple hours after high tide, during the two days before or after a full or new moon! At its peak, the sand can be covered with thousands of the little critters, and collecting grunions to fry up a late-night snack is a favorite San Diego pastime (no collection is allowed in April through June, and note that a fishing license is required to scoop up the fish).

wildlife.ca.gov/Fishing/Ocean/Grunion
Neighborhoods: Ocean Beach, Mission Beach, La Jolla Shores, Coronado Beach, and Silver Strand

BLOOM WITH SPRING WILDFLOWERS
IN THE ANZA-BORREGO DESERT

Each spring, arid Anza-Borrego Desert State Park blooms with a feast of color and fragrance as the annual wildflower show arrives for a short, sometimes spectacular display. The state park, two hours east of San Diego, is the largest in California. Its 600,000 acres include palm oases, slot canyons, rugged mountains, colorful badlands, and 110 miles of hiking trails. Amid this austere beauty, the diversity and quantity of the annual bloom depends on a cool winter and solid rainfall. Once or twice a decade conditions align, and a “super bloom” comes along to flood Instagram screens with vast carpets of yellow, purple, and pink wildflowers. Small patches typically start to appear in February, but the peak of the show—which might last only a week or two—usually falls in March. Make Mother Nature proud by sticking to the marked trails and don’t pick the flowers!

200 Palm Canyon Dr., Borrego Springs, East San Diego County
760-767-4684 or 760-767-5311
parks.ca.gov/?page_id=638

STROLL THE OCEANSIDE PIER

Spend a day in Oceanside, San Diego County's third-largest community, easily reached in an hour from downtown via frequent Amtrak or Coaster service. It's a half-mile walk from the station down to the Oceanside Pier, one of the longest wooden piers on the West Coast. Hundreds of fishermen line the pier every morning to compete with pelicans and harbor seals for the abundant fish swimming between the submerged pillars. Oceanside's beachfront extends for three miles and is home to international surfing competitions, endurance events, and outrigger races. But if you feel like getting in on the action you can rent a bike, kayak, or paddle board, or join in on a beach volleyball game. There are several casual restaurants near the pier entry, and the Oceanside Farmers Market takes place nearby on Thursday mornings from 9:00 a.m. to 1:00 p.m.

North Pacific St., Oceanside, 800-350-7873
visitoceanside.org

ROAM COASTAL ROCKS
AND DISCOVER TIDE POOLS

Although San Diego boasts about 70 miles of beachfront, there are a number of rocky coastal stretches that invite us to observe the intertidal ecosystems, where the land greets the sea. At low tide, when the seawater recedes, pockets and channels in the rock reveal small pools inhabited by a variety of creatures. One of the best spots is Point Loma's sandstone cliffs, below the Cabrillo Lighthouse. Barnacles and mussels abound, but keep an eye out for starfish, shore crabs, anemones, California sea hares, lobsters, and even the dark red Pacific octopus. If you're lucky, the vivid nudibranchs can be a spectacular sighting. Other great locations include the Ocean Beach Pier, Tourmaline Surf Park, La Jolla cliffs between the Children's Pool and the Cove, and South Cardiff State Beach. November through March are optimal for tide pooling, when the tide is low during daylight hours.

Coastal locations throughout San Diego

TIP

Be sure to check the daily tide report, and note that collection of natural or living organisms at tide pools is strictly prohibited. Wear footwear with good grip and that you don't mind getting wet (a change of clothes and shoes is nice to have).

LIFT OFF
IN A HOT AIR BALLOON

Soaring silently across the rolling countryside is a fantasy for many of us, and San Diego's north county region offers two options for flights in a hot air balloon. Liftoffs happen at dawn in Temecula Valley, an hour north of downtown, transiting rural country scenes of rambling ranch houses, citrus trees, and vineyards—in winter, snow-topped mountains serve as a backdrop. Or, take off on a Champagne flight just before dusk along the Cardiff coastline, 30 minutes from downtown, and survey the farms and posh estates of Rancho Santa Fe and Carmel Valley as the breeze carries you gently inland. With Compass Balloons, the exact takeoff location is determined the day before, based on winds and other conditions, and a maximum of eight passengers are aboard group flights (private charters available).

969 Villa Cardiff Dr., Cardiff, 760-704-7407
31867 Rancho California Rd., Temecula, 760-704-7407
compassballoons.com

TIP

Dedicated and amateur balloonatics congregate for the annual Temecula Balloon & Wine Festival, held on a weekend around June 1. Concerts, wine tastings, and—of course—mass balloon launches (and rides) are part of the festivities: 951-676-6713, tvbwf.com.

NAVIGATE WRECK ALLEY

Although the Southern California coastline is famed for its towering kelp forests, another thrill for divers is Wreck Alley, so named for the ship carcasses collecting right off the shores of Mission Beach. The headliner is the HMCS *Yukon*, a 366-foot Canadian destroyer escort that was sunk in 2000. Intact and sitting underwater between 70 and 100 feet, the wreck is home to plenty of marine life, with swim-throughs and penetration opportunities. Nearby is the *Ruby E.*, a weathered, 166-foot Coast Guard cutter lying upright about 80 feet down, and the NOSC Tower, an anemone-encrusted research installation appearing much like a small oil rig and reaching within 30 feet of the surface. Waterhorse Charters takes scuba-certified divers here and to other top sites, such as the Point Loma kelp forests and the Islas los Coronados off Tijuana.

1617 Quivira Rd., Ste. B, Mission Bay
619-224-6195 or 858-800-4860
waterhorsecharters.com

69

ANGLE FOR A BITE
ON A SPORTFISHING TRIP

Once known as the "tuna capital of the world," San Diego is also one of the birthplaces of modern saltwater sportfishing. The harbor nurtures a massive sportfishing industry, with charters ranging from half- and full-day to overnight trips reaching fishing grounds up to 100 miles offshore. On close-in trips, morning and afternoon departures target yellowtail, bass, barracuda, rockfish, bonito, and tuna, while multi-day journeys reach remote islands off Baja where catches of yellowfin tuna and wahoo more than 100 pounds are regularly taken. H&M Landing and Point Loma Sportfishing handle scheduled and chartered trips on a variety of different boats equipped with state-of-the-art fish finders. They'll rent tackle and gear, set you up with a California fishing license or Mexican permit, and refer you to processing services to have your catch processed and frozen in convenient fillets.

Point Loma Sportfishing
1403 Scott St., Point Loma, 619-223-1627
pointlomasportfishing.com

H&M Landing
2803 Emerson St., Point Loma, 619-222-1144
hmlanding.com

BEHOLD THE CALIFORNIA COASTLINE AT TORREY PINES

The 300-foot-high seafront cliffs rising from beaches north of La Jolla are home to Torrey Pines Natural State Reserve, a 1,500-acre park that shelters North America's rarest pine trees. Found only here and on a small island 175 miles northwest, the trees are inelegant and gnarled characters clinging precariously to water-carved sandstone bluffs. The reserve is also one of the last parcels of precious, undeveloped southern California coastline, encompassing the beach below and a lagoon immediately north. Wildlife includes red-tailed hawk, California quail, black-tailed jackrabbits, and coyotes. On fog-shrouded spring mornings visitors are rewarded with a dazzle of wildflowers. Stop by the visitor center, an old adobe brick lodge inspired by Hopi dwellings, to get info on a half-dozen trails up to 1.4 miles in length.

12600 N Torrey Pines Rd., Torrey Pines, 858-755-2063
torreypine.org

TIP

A few restrictions are in place to help preserve the reserve. No food is allowed at Torrey Pines except on the beach near the entrance, where there are trashcans. Smoking, dogs, and drones are also not allowed.

71

CYCLE THE BAYSHORE BIKEWAY

Many of San Diego's cycling routes involve hills, but the 24-mile Bayshore Bikeway offers a flat, breezy trip around San Diego Bay, and most of it is on dedicated paths, away from traffic. You can ride the horseshoe-shaped circuit in either direction, but I recommend picking up a hybrid, road, or electric bike downtown at Wheel Fun Rentals and taking the ferry over to Coronado, looping counter-clockwise around the bay (Wheel Fun also has a location in Coronado). Wend your way through resort-y Coronado past the iconic Hotel Del Coronado to the Silver Strand, an isthmus of dunes linking the island to Imperial Beach, California's southernmost beach community. At the southern end of the bay, the hills of Tijuana float on the horizon, while the water sparkles like diamonds, courtesy of the salt crystals harvested here. Circling north, you'll pass a national wildlife refuge, the naval shipyard, and colorful murals at Chicano Park.

1355 N Harbor Dr., 619-342-7244
Neighborhoods: Downtown, Coronado, and Chula Vista
wheelfunrentals.com

TIP

Avid cyclists can complete the circuit in a couple of hours, but casual riders will want to allow most of the day for the journey back to downtown. Alternatively, a counterclockwise route will allow you to hop onto the San Diego Trolley at the Palomar Street Transit Center, shaving off the last 10 miles.

Mission Basilica San Diego deAlcalá

CULTURE AND HISTORY

SEE A FUTURE TONY WINNER AT LA JOLLA PLAYHOUSE

With more than 150 stages, San Diego is a premiere destination for theater, sending more shows to Broadway than any other city in America. Many of them originate at the La Jolla Playhouse, internationally celebrated for creating some of the most exciting work in American theater. The Playhouse boasts a Hollywood pedigree—it was founded in 1947 by Gregory Peck, Dorothy McGuire, and Mel Ferrer—but it regularly sends shows to Broadway, and they return home clutching Tony Awards. Forty-two of these statues have been earned to date, for such long-running hits as *Big River*, *The Who's Tommy*, *Jersey Boys*, and *Come from Away*. Situated on the campus of the University of California–San Diego, the playhouse encompasses four venues, including the main, 492-seat, proscenium-style Mandell Weiss Theatre.

2910 La Jolla Village Dr., La Jolla, 858-550-1010
lajollaplayhouse.org

HOIST NAUTICAL HISTORY AT THE MARITIME MUSEUM OF SAN DIEGO

As befits one of America's great sailing harbors, San Diego is home to a world-class maritime museum with a collection of historic vessels. The fleet, docked at the Embarcadero, includes the HMS *Surprise* (featured in the Oscar-winning film *Master and Commander*), the 1898 steam ferry *Berkeley*, and the Soviet-era Russian submarine *B-39*. The star of the show is the world's oldest active ship, *Star of India*, dating to 1863 and newly refurbished in 2020. There are rewarding exhibits on board each vessel offering hands-on family-friendly experiences. Better yet, sign up for a four-hour circuit of San Diego Bay aboard the historic small vessel *Californian*, a replica of a gold rush–era cutter and the Official Tall Ship of the State of California, or aboard the *San Salvador,* a replica of Cabrillo's ship that arrived in the bay in 1542.

1492 N Harbor Dr., downtown, 619-234-9153
sdmaritime.org

74

CHANNEL MASTERFUL ARCHITECTURE
AT THE SALK INSTITUTE

After developing the polio vaccine, Jonas Salk sought to create a collaborative research environment. In 1960 the City of San Diego gifted Salk with 27 prime acres overlooking the Pacific Ocean, and he partnered with architect Louis Kahn to design a research center "worthy of a visit by Picasso." The resulting Salk Institute is one of the most important architectural works in the US: austere structures of concrete, teak, lead, glass, and steel that provide open and unobstructed laboratory spaces to foster teamwork. A single, striking water feature unites the buildings—the sun sets along its axis during the spring and fall equinoxes. Surprisingly few visitors seek out San Diego's architectural masterpiece, but it's an essential stop for anyone interested in modern design. Hour-long guided tours are available Wednesday through Friday at 10:00 and 11:30 a.m. and can be booked online.

10010 N Torrey Pines Rd., Torrey Pines, 858-453-4100
salk.edu/about/visiting-salk

INHALE THE VIEW
AT CABRILLO NATIONAL MONUMENT

San Diego's best viewpoint is revealed at this national monument, located 422 feet above sea level at the tip of Point Loma, the muscular peninsula that dominates the entrance to San Diego Bay. You'll spot the hills of Tijuana, nuclear submarines at Naval Base Point Loma, and—on clear days—the mountainous backcountry that ruffles the horizon 50 miles inland. In winter months gray whales can be spotted offshore, and in spring wildflowers add drops of color. The breathtaking views serve as a backdrop for the early history of San Diego, which began when Portuguese explorer Juan Rodríguez Cabrillo discovered the bay in 1542. A restored 1855 lighthouse illustrates the lonely life of lightkeepers, and a small museum tells about gun batteries established on the peninsula during WWII, when San Diego served as headquarters for the Pacific Fleet.

1800 Cabrillo Memorial Dr., Point Loma, 619-523-4285
nps.gov/cabr

OPEN THE DOOR
TO THE MUSEUMS OF BALBOA PARK

Even if one ignores the presence of the San Diego Zoo, Balboa Park represents one of the most vital urban cultural parks in the nation. Seventeen museums and cultural institutions cover a diverse range of subjects, from San Diego history to the development of flight, trains, and automobiles, to the artistry of the old masters. And proving that the park's museums continue to grow and diversify, the Comic-Con Museum opened in 2021 to explore the world of comics and related popular arts. Don't overlook the park's architecture—the romantic, flamboyant Spanish-Renaissance façades along the Prado were built in 1915 for the Panama-California Exposition. The Pan American Plaza, created for a subsequent 1935 exposition, showcases styles ranging from Mexican Pueblo to Art Deco. Save money with the multi-museum Balboa Park pass, valid for one, seven, or 365 days (but not accepted at the Zoo or Comic-Con Museum).

1549 El Prado, Balboa Park, 619-239-0512
balboapark.org/explore/museums

TIP

Keep in mind that the Zoo requires most of a day to tour, so you'll want to plan at least a second day in the park for the museums, gardens, and hiking trails.

TOP MUSEUMS OF BALBOA PARK

Fleet Science Center
1875 El Prado
619-238-1233
rhfleet.org

Museum of Photographic Arts
1649 El Prado
619-232-7931
mopa.org

San Diego Air & Space Museum
2001 Pan American Plaza
619-234-8291
sandiegoairandspace.org

San Diego Automotive Museum
2080 Pan American Plaza
619-231-2886
sdautomuseum.org

San Diego History Center
1649 El Prado
619-232-6203
sandiegohistory.org

San Diego Model Railroad Museum
1649 El Prado
619-696-0199
sdmrm.org

Museum of Us
1350 El Prado
619-239-2001
museumofus.org

The Nat (San Diego Natural History Museum)
1788 El Prado
877-946-7797
sdnhm.org

San Diego Museum of Art
1450 El Prado
619-232-7931
sdmart.org

Timken Museum of Art
1500 El Prado
619-239-5548
timkenmuseum.org

LET THE WAVES ROCK YOU TO SLEEP AT CRYSTAL PIER HOTEL

Trouble getting a good night's rest? You'll be lulled to sleep when you surf over to this cluster of cottages sitting literally right above the waves on Pacific Beach's vintage Crystal Pier. Each of the 24 Cape Cod–style cottages sleeps two to six and offers separate living room and bedroom, fully equipped kitchen, and private patio with breathtaking ocean views. The sound of waves is soothing, and the pier sways gently with each passing swell. The whitewashed walls of these sweet, blue-shuttered cottages date to 1936, but all have been renovated (six additional rooms are found in the pier's entrance on the "mainland"). The boardwalk action is only a few steps (and worlds) away, and the views of sunsets and surfers are delicious. Guests drive right out and park beside their cottages, a real boon on crowded weekends. The accommodations book up fast; reserve months in advance for summer and holiday weekends.

4500 Ocean Blvd., Pacific Beach, 800-748-5894 or 858-483-6983
crystalpier.com

PROWL THE LEGENDARY HOTEL DEL CORONADO

"The Del," as it's affectionately known, is the epitome of a grand old seaside hotel, built in 1888 on a sandy isle across from San Diego's then-young downtown. This national historic landmark—immortalized in the classic comedy *Some Like it Hot*, flaunts turn-of-the-century Victorian opulence, defined by red turrets, soaring cupolas, and gingerbread trim. Presidents, royalty, and celebrities have stayed at the Del over the years, and Wizard of Oz author L. Frank Baum so loved the resort that its architecture inspired cover artwork for the Oz series. It's usually packed to its rafters with tourists and wedding parties, so you'll pay an arm and a leg to bunk here. You can explore most of the public areas independently, but if you want a more in-depth look at the history of this iconic landmark, spring for the 90-minute guided tour, conducted daily at 10:00 a.m. (and on weekends at 2:00 p.m.). There's also a Haunted Tour nightly at 7:00 p.m. with stories of the Del's notorious phantom Kate Morgan.

1500 Orange Ave., Coronado, 619-522-8100
hoteldel.com

DEPLOY AMERICAN NAVAL HISTORY

ABOARD THE USS *MIDWAY*

In 2004, following a 47-year history that began one week after the Japanese surrender ending WWII, the USS *Midway* made her final voyage into San Diego Bay. By the time the aircraft carrier was decommissioned in 1992, the *Midway* had served in the Vietnam War, operated as the flagship for Desert Storm, and evacuated 1,800 people from Subic Bay Naval Base in the Philippines when it was threatened by volcanic eruption. In all, more than 200,000 men served aboard the aircraft carrier, which was for 10 years the largest vessel as sea. Today, the *Midway* is a fascinating naval museum drawing more than a million visitors annually. A self-guided audio tour takes visitors to several levels of the *Midway*, telling the story of life on board, but the highlight is climbing the superstructure to the bridge and gazing down on the 1,001-foot-long flight deck, with various aircraft poised for duty.

910 N Harbor Dr., downtown, 619-544-9600
midway.org

PICTURE ART ALIVE
AT THE SAN DIEGO MUSEUM OF ART

For one glorious spring weekend each year since 1982, the San Diego Museum of Art has been transformed for its signature annual event, a series of about 80 living tableaux that reinterpret some of the museum's masterpieces in flowers—a union of paint and plant. The weekend starts with a major fundraiser, the Bloom Bash, a party where the floral interpretations are debuted, with their inspirations from the permanent collection—both sculptures and paintings—parked just behind. The interior rotunda is converted into a giant, two-story sculpture of plants and flowers. A mix of the literal and abstract, and the whimsical and contemplative, the April event is the museum's major fundraiser for the year and draws up to 12,000 visitors over the three days before coming down on Sunday evening.

1450 El Prado, Balboa Park, 619-232-7931
sdmart.org

COMMUNE WITH PINNIPEDS

AT THE CHILDREN'S POOL

If you thought politics in Washington DC was divisive, wait till you get a load of the backstory at the Children's Pool, arguably the most contentious piece of real estate in posh La Jolla. The jetty-protected cove was created in 1932 to provide a safe harbor for young children to swim. But since the 1990s, harbor seals have adopted this choice setting, using it as a rookery for their pups. From mid-December to mid-May the beach is closed to humans, when as many as 200 seals can be viewed lazing in the sun and taking dips in the sea. The community remains sharply divided over retaking what is now called Casa Beach for the diaper-clad set, while courts have sided with the easy-going seals. Meanwhile, it's an accessible glimpse into San Diego's marine ecology, with docents from the Sierra Club providing useful insight.

850 Coast Blvd., La Jolla
sealconservancy.org

TIP

On occasion harbor seals vacate the cove, but you'll probably find them, along with yelping sea lions, on the bluffs and caves just north. Those kayaking from La Jolla Shores get prime encounters.

FLOCK TO THE LIVING COAST DISCOVERY CENTER

Established to protect rare wildlife, the San Diego Bay National Wildlife Refuge encompasses much of the southern end of the bay, bordered on the east by Chula Vista. These intertidal mudflat and coastal salt marsh habitats are home to four endangered or threatened species, but more than 200 species of birds have been observed at the marsh, an important wintering area for many shorebirds. Located on the Sweetwater Marsh Unit of the refuge, the Living Coast Discovery Center is aimed at guests of all ages, inviting us to explore the region's flora and fauna. The nonprofit zoo and aquarium offers hands-on exhibits and up close encounters with plant and animal species native to Southern California coastal habitats, and there are daily feeding presentations with endangered green sea turtles, stingrays, leopard sharks, and American bald and golden eagles. The center's large collection of raptors also includes hawks, falcons, owls, an American bald eagle, a golden eagle, and more.

1000 Gunpowder Point Dr., Chula Vista, 619-409-5900
thelivingcoast.org

CHEER THE BARD
AT THE OLD GLOBE THEATRE

One of the country's leading professional regional theaters, the Tony-winning Old Globe is a complex of three performance venues located inside Balboa Park. Though it is best known for the 580-seat Old Globe—fashioned after Shakespeare's Globe Theatre in London—there are also the 250-seat Sheryl and Harvey White Theatre and the 580-seat open-air Lowell Davies Festival Theatre, which is used for summer Shakespeare performances under the stars. The Globe mounts 15 productions each year, from world premieres of such subsequent Broadway hits as *The Full Monty* and *Into the Woods* to the Christmas perennial, *Dr. Seuss' How the Grinch Stole Christmas!*, a popular family draw during the holidays since 1997. Note that parking is not adjacent to the Globe—allow an hour to locate parking and walk to the theaters.

1363 Old Globe Way, Balboa Park, 619-234–5623
theoldglobe.org

FERRY TO BEAUTIFUL CORONADO ISLAND

Although Coronado is more of a peninsula connected by a narrow spit of sand, it does indeed have an island-y, resort ambience, and it's a swell day trip by ferry from San Diego just across the bay. The ferry service departs from two downtown locations: every 30 minutes from the foot of Fifth Avenue (behind the convention center) or on the hour from the Broadway Pier, next to the USS *Midway*. The 10-minute crossing plants you at the Coronado Ferry Landing, where you'll find restaurants, shops, art galleries, free concerts on weekends, and a farmers market on Tuesdays. You can also rent a bike or surrey and cycle over to Orange Avenue, Coronado's charming downtown, and on to the historic Hotel del Coronado, 1.5 miles away. The shoreline fronting the hotel, Coronado Beach, is one of San Diego's finest.

600 Convention Way, 619-234-4111
90 N Harbor Dr., 619-234-4111
Neighborhoods: Downtown, Coronado
coronadoferrylanding.com

DISCOVER THE BIRTHPLACE
OF SAN DIEGO IN OLD TOWN

San Diego was home to the original European settlement on the West Coast, where Franciscan Father Junípero Serra established San Diego de Alcalá, the first of 21 California missions. The small settlement that grew below the mission is where the community began in the early 1800s. Old Town San Diego State Historic Park has been restored to highlight life in early California, the Mexican-American period between 1821 and 1872. You'll find a schoolhouse, blacksmith's shop, newspaper office, stables, and more, all surrounding a central plaza. Free walking tours are offered daily at 11:00 a.m. and 2:00 p.m. There are restaurants and strolling mariachi bands at Fiesta de Reyes, a charming shopping complex inhabiting a 1930s-era motel built in the adobe style, and many more Mexican eateries and shops can be found outside the park along San Diego Avenue.

4002 Wallace St., Old Town, 619-220-5422
oldtownsandiego.org

CLAMBER DOWN
TO LA JOLLA'S SUNNY JIM SEA CAVE

Perched on bluffs just east of La Jolla Cove, the Cave Store shelters a secret passageway: A constricted, eerie tunnel descends under the store down 144 steps to a wood-plank observation deck opening onto the sea. The tunnel to the cave was hand-carved by two laborers in 1903 using picks and shovels, creating an early tourist attraction for the community. Sunny Jim is one of seven sea caves otherwise accessed only by kayak (or long swim). The cave got its name years later, when L. Frank Baum, author of *The Wizard of Oz*, said the cave's opening looked like a British cereal mascot named Sunny Jim. Over time, the cave was also used by smugglers, who would bring ashore alcohol and immigrants. Kids love this spooky experience—hold the handrail and your little ones' hands tightly.

1325 Coast Blvd., La Jolla, 858-459-0746
cavestore.com

FIND YOUR GREEN THUMB
IN THE GARDENS OF BALBOA PARK

The development of Balboa Park's extensive, mature botanical collection is thanks largely to Kate Sessions, a horticulturalist who devoted her life to transforming the park's desolate mesas and scrub-filled canyons. Stop by the much-photographed Lily Pond and Botanical Building, built for the 1915–16 Exposition and subject of a $28 million renovation in 2025—it's one of the largest lath structures in the world. Inside, the collection includes cycads, ferns, orchids, carnivorous plants, and tropical palms. Across Park Boulevard (past the Natural History Museum) lies the Desert Garden, containing cacti, succulents, and drought-resistant plants (peak blooms January through March). Immediately next door is the Inez Grant Parker Memorial Rose Garden, with 1,600 roses covering more than 130 varieties, with blooms peaking in April and May. The 12-acre Japanese Friendship Garden requires admission but features centuries-old gardening techniques adapted to San Diego's climate, along with stone arrangements, koi ponds, and sukiya-style buildings.

1549 El Prado, Balboa Park, 619-239-0512
balboapark.org/explore/gardens

SKETCH YOURSELF
INTO THE SCENE AT COMIC-CON

Every year, for one long July weekend San Diego becomes the center of the comic-lover's universe. Since 1970, when the very first Comic-Con convention was organized, the nonprofit event has grown to draw more than 135,000 attendees to the San Diego Convention Center. The event typically sells out the day tickets go on sale—*eight* months in advance! Luring comic-book fans, sci-fi geeks, cosplayers, pop-culture buffs, and bystanders alike, the event has been transformed into a multimedia sensation that incorporates all genres of collectibles, toys, and games. Most attendees are hoping for a coveted seat in at least one of the Hall H showcases, where people like George Lucas, Ryan Reynolds, and their ilk preview their latest projects. Even from the sidelines, Comic-Con is a people-watching bonanza, where enthusiasts dressed in wild costumes can parade in a judgement-free universe. A substantial Hollywood contingent also comes to launch the latest fantasy, horror, sci-fi, and animated products—the sneak previews of movies and TV shows headed to large and small screens alike are often attended by some of the biggest celebrities.

111 W Harbor Dr., downtown, 619-491-2475
comic-con.org

TIP

Pop culture now has a permanent home with the opening of the Comic-Con Museum in Balboa Park. The museum offers permanent and rotating exhibits, film screenings in a state-of-the-art theater, and a Character Hall of Fame.

DAYTRIP TO PALOMAR OBSERVATORY

Situated at an elevation of 5,598 feet atop Palomar Mountain, the highest point in San Diego County, this observatory for several decades housed the world's largest telescope. It was funded by a $6 million grant from Caltech in 1928, but it took two decades—following trial-and-error fabrication of the 200-inch reflecting mirror in Corning, New York—before the Hale Telescope was finally employed to survey the skies. Many discoveries have been made, and researchers continue to study near-Earth asteroids, outer solar system planets, star formation, black holes, quasars, and much more. The 135-foot-high dome containing the telescope is a beautifully understated Art Deco structure with balanced proportions that dominates the surrounding forest. It's located 65 miles from downtown, and self-guided tours are possible most days, but the observatory also offers one-hour guided tours on weekends, from April through October. Check the weather conditions before visiting, especially in winter.

35899 Canfield Rd., Palomar, 760-742-2119
Neighborhood: Palomar Mountain
astro.caltech.edu/palomar/

TIP

The quirky, adjacent mountain community of Palomar has a campground, grocery store, restaurant, and post office.

PICNIC AT A FREE OUTDOOR CONCERT
AT THE SPRECKELS ORGAN PAVILION

Donated to the citizens of San Diego in 1914 by brothers John D. and Adolph Spreckels, this ornate, curved pavilion houses a magnificent organ with 4,518 individual pipes—it's the largest outdoor musical instrument in the world. The pipes range in length from the size of a pencil to more than 32 feet. With only brief interruptions, the organ has been in continuous use for more than a century, and today you can enjoy free hour-long concerts on Sundays at 2:00 p.m., rain or shine, given by San Diego Civic Organist Raúl Prieto Ramírez, the only full-time municipal organist in the world. Additional concerts are scheduled on Mondays at 7:30 p.m. from late June to the end of August and on other evenings throughout the year. There's seating for 2,400 but little shade, so bring an umbrella on warm days, or on the rare drizzly afternoon.

El Prado, Balboa Park, 619-702-8138
spreckelsorgan.org

PAY TRIBUTE
TO MISSION BASILICA SAN DIEGO DE ALCALÁ

Originally established above Old Town, this was the first link in what became a chain of 21 California missions. They were founded by Father Junípero Serra, a Spanish priest charged with spreading Christianity to the native inhabitants of the New World. In 1774, the mission was moved to its present site, just up the valley, where agricultural prospects were better, on a rise that offered views onto the surrounding marshes, plains, and mesas. A dam built just upriver was probably the first irrigation project in the West, allowing Serra's flock to grow wheat, barley, vineyards, olives, and dates. Also noteworthy: In using adobe for walls and clay-tile roofs, Father Serra inspired a long list of 20th-century architects to adopt the same style in structures throughout California for decades to come. You can worship at the birthplace of Christianity on the West Coast; Mass is held daily for the active parish.

10818 San Diego Mission Rd., Mission Valley, 619-281-8449
missionsandiego.org

TIP

Other missions near San Diego include Mission San Antonia de Pala near Mount Palomar, and Mission Santa Ysabel near Julian. Known as "the King of Missions," Mission San Luis Rey de Francia in Oceanside is the largest of California's missions and one of its most beautiful.

Bazaar del Mundo

SHOPPING AND FASHION

SUPPORT ORIGINAL ART
AT SPANISH VILLAGE ART CENTER

Occupying a cluster of 36 low-slung, ramshackle bungalows just south of the San Diego Zoo, the Spanish Village Art Center is a working-artists' collective. The charming buildings were meant to be temporary, housing restaurants and shops for the 1935–36 expo. But just before demolition, local artists approached the city and proposed to convert the village into working art studios and provide community outreach. The artists gained an affordable place to work and sell their art, and they frequently open their studio doors to allow the public to watch the creative process. The artists—more than 200—come from a variety of backgrounds and places, and include award-winning painters, sculptors, metalsmiths, jewelry designers, photographers, and printmakers. Artists are found creating beautiful pieces in their Village studios on any given day, but the center hums with activity on weekends.

1770 Village Place, Balboa Park, 619 233-9050
spanishvillageart.com

REVEAL YOUR INNER DESIGNER INSTINCTS
ALONG CEDROS AVENUE

An eclectic mélange of more than 85 indie shops, boutiques, and galleries packed into a few short blocks, the Cedros Avenue Design District is a treasure trove of designer goods. Some of the vendors are housed in a row of Quonset huts that were constructed in the 1950s for a defense contractor who made spy plane photographic equipment and other gear. Today, at Solo, more than two dozen independently curated stores sell chic furniture, original art and photography, home decor, and clothing. Other shops feature local artisans and designers, with a healthy focus on products that are fair trade and ethically sourced. There are cafés, a brewery, an olive oil purveyor, and on Sundays, a farmers market blossoms from noon to 4 p.m. Bonus: The Coaster station is next door, making Cedros Avenue an easy trip from downtown.

S. Cedros Ave., Solana Beach, 858-755-0444
cedrosavenue.com

BROWSE WITH TIJUANEROS
AT LAS AMERICAS PREMIUM OUTLETS

San Diego's largest outlet mall, Las Americas is more than the sum of its 190 stores. The mall sits 20 minutes south of downtown, literally a stone's throw from the border crossing into Tijuana, Mexico. As a result, the mall attracts a diverse crowd from both sides of *la frontera*, all in search of bargains from the name brands hanging their outlet flags: Ann Taylor, Armani Exchange, Disney, Hugo, Michael Kors, The North Face, Polo, and Tommy Hilfiger. It's an oddly positive cultural experience at the crossroads of two countries, with "the Wall" looming just 100 feet away. Achiote Restaurant next door offers authentic Mexican breakfast, lunch, and dinner (try the chilaquiles). Las Americas is easily reached via the San Diego Trolley—the San Ysidro stop is just a 10-minute walk from the entrance.

4211 Camino de la Plaza, San Ysidro, 619-934-8400
San Diego–Tijuana border crossing
premiumoutlets.com/outlet/las-americas

TIP

Carlsbad Premium Outlets is the other major outlet mall for the San Diego area, located 40 minutes north of downtown. Unique brands worth seeking out include Ferragamo, Le Creuset, Prana, Tory Birch, Tumi, and Zwilling.

PICK A COLOR, ANY COLOR, AT PIGMENT

More than a gift shop, Pigment is a beautifully curated lifestyle boutique that sells much of the homeware and personal apparel you might expect—candles, cards, T-shirts, novelties—but the emporium carves a unique niche in at least two ways. First, Pigment is organized by color. So, you don't look for candles in any one section—you'll find them positioned around the store, arranged by color. While this might frustrate those looking for a specific item quickly, it gently nurtures our inner shopping bug. Second, the store hosts a terrarium-building area, for those looking to come away with a one-of-a-kind keepsake or gift. Pick a glass orb and marry it with any of the dozens of succulents and accents (rocks, moss, colored sand) on offer. Pigment provides planting medium and all the supplies and table space for creating right in the store. In addition, you'll find fun children's clothing, cookbooks, bartending supplies, perfumes, accent pillows, and other merchandise, much of it hand-sourced from local artists.

3801 30th St., North Park, 619-501-6318
2885 Perry Rd., Liberty Station, 619-795-6300
3715 Caminito Court, Del Mar, 858-876-6360
shoppigment.com

96

OGLE FAMED AUTHORS AT WARWICK'S

Other cities may have bigger, more trendy, more niche options for stocking bookshelves, but Warwick's is the oldest family-owned and continuously operated bookstore in the United States. Founded in 1896, this La Jolla institution has a knowledgeable staff that stays abreast of local authors, and its roots in the local community go deep. Over the years, Warwick's has hosted countless world-class writers on book tours (many at off-site events), such as Barbara Kingsolver, Isabelle Allende, Kirk Douglas, David Sedaris, Alice Walker, Hillary Clinton, and Margaret Thatcher . . . from presidents and senators to Pulitzer Prize winners and celebrities, they've all been here. But even when a bestselling author isn't in the house, count on about 25,000 titles to peruse and purchase, and in addition to books you'll find San Diego's best stationery store, with choice office supplies and other gifts on offer.

7812 Girard Ave, La Jolla, 858-454-0347
warwicks.com

SURRENDER TO YOUR SHOPPING HABIT AT WESTFIELD UTC

Okay, so "UTC"—formerly University Towne Centre—isn't the sexiest name, but this large outdoor shopping center recently completed a major renovation and expansion and stands today as San Diego's swankiest mall. UTC epitomizes California living, and with more than 150 stores plus dozens of other services, it has become a centerpiece of consumerism in the greater La Jolla area. Anchor stores include Macy's and Nordstrom, while venues such as Hermès, Le Labo, Polestar, and Aesop draw more discerning types. There's an ice-skating rink, a multilevel 24-Hour Fitness facility, and an AMC Cinema with 14 screens and stadium-style seating. Dining is a big attraction at a variety of price points, with places like Din Tai Fung (Taiwan soup dumplings), Pazza (homemade sausage and pastas), and L55 (designer tacos) keeping visitors happy and sated well into the evening.

4545 La Jolla Village Dr., La Jolla, 858-546-8858
westfield.com/en/united-states/utc

BUY SOUTH OF THE BORDER WITHOUT A PASSPORT

AT BAZAAR DEL MUNDO

Tijuana is just a 20-minute drive from downtown San Diego. But why fight border traffic on the return when you can take in south-of-the-border style at Bazaar del Mundo? This meticulously curated collection of boutiques offers an array of kitchenware, such as vivid tablecloths, hand blown glassware, and Talaverra dishes; party goods like artisan-crafted piñatas, ornaments, toys, and dolls; and festive Mexican folk art, Guatemalan textiles, Mata Ortiz pottery, and Navaho jewelry. Although you won't find the bargains prevalent on the other side of the border, the goods are generally of higher quality. There isn't a more colorful place to browse in San Diego, and if you get hungry wander next door for tacos and tamales at Casa Guadalajara.

4133 Taylor St., Old Town, 619-296-3161
bazaardelmundo.com

TIP

As an alternative, Artelexia embraces a pop upcycling aesthetic by cleverly repurposing frugal Mexican products to create items of cheerful beauty, such as handmade shadow boxes known as *nichos*. Much of the folk art is sourced from Oaxaca—feel free to explore with a *paleta* (popsicle) in hand.

3803 Ray St., North Park, 619-501-6381
artelexia.com

EMBARK ON A RETAIL THERAPY JOURNEY
IN MISSION VALLEY

Consumer central for San Diegans is Mission Valley. For one mile, on either side of the slender San Diego River, two of the city's biggest outdoor malls provide nearly three million square feet of retail space. Mission Valley is the older of the two, hosting stores aimed at bargain-hunters such as Target, Bloomingdale's Outlet Store, and Nordstrom Rack. You'll also find a 20-screen AMC movie theater and more than 100 other stores and places to eat. Across the streets north and west are separate complexes that feature additional stores. The more upscale Fashion Valley has four anchor tenants: Macy's, Neiman Marcus, Nordstrom, and Bloomingdale's, plus high-end stores like Prada, Apple, Gucci, Christian Louboutin, and 200 others. There are several solid restaurants and another 18-screen AMC theater, plus smaller malls just east of Highway 163.

Mission Valley: 1640 Camino Del Rio N., San Diego, 619-296-6375
mission-valley.com

Fashion Valley: 7007 Friars Rd., San Diego, 619-297-3381
simon.com/mall/fashion-valley

TIP

Both shopping centers are easily accessible via San Diego Trolley. Take the Green Line from downtown, Old Town, or East County. The malls are just a two-minute walk from the same-named stops on the Green Line.

AMBLE THROUGH THE BOUTIQUES
OF LA JOLLA

Nicknamed "The Jewel," the village of La Jolla is ideal for shoppers as well as strolling couples, people-watchers, and anyone who enjoys the sea air and glimpses of the roiled coastline. You'll find a few name brands, but mostly these are one-of-a-kind boutiques, ranging from haute couture to the comfortably familiar. The best shopping is concentrated along fashionable Prospect Street (which some refer to as San Diego's Rodeo Drive), and on three avenues abutting it: Ivanhoe, Herschel, and Girard. Look for fine jewelry, luxury watches, and estate pieces at CJ Charles; America's longest-running family-owned bookstore (Warwick's); collectible prints from Authentic Vintage Posters; San Diego's best toy store (Geppetto's); and some of San Diego's favorite restaurants, more than enough for a full day of retail R&R.

858-230-2725
Neighborhood: La Jolla
lajollabythesea.com

Go Local at the Hillcrest Farmers Market and Open-Air Bazaar

Balboa Park

SUGGESTED ITINERARIES

ACTIVE OUTDOOR ADVENTURES

CULTURAL AFFAIRS

ESSENTIAL SAN DIEGO

FAMILY FUN

FOOD FINDS

LIQUID LIBATIONS

FREEBIES

HISTORY LESSONS

ROMANTIC RENDEZVOUS

SPORTS SPOTS

Comic-Con

ACTIVITIES
BY SEASON

SPRING

SUMMER

FALL

WINTER

INDEX